The Volunteer

by Shane Paul O'Doherty

Strategic Book Group

Strategic Book Group
P.O. Box 333
Durham CT 06422
www.StrategicBookClub.com

ISBN 978-1-61204-528-3

Book Design: Linda W. Rigsbee

Table of Contents

Preface

It has not been easy to write this book. The subject-matter is so contentious that it will satisfy few and annoy many. I have not set out to write a political, sociological or historical study, but a personal recollection. I have resisted the temptation to exploit the advantages of retrospection and research to paint myself as more aware or mature than I actually was. I hope that my story will move people to believe that the need for a negotiated peace was greater than the need for a pyrrhic victory by any party to the Northern Ireland troubles. There is always a path to peace if only we will take it.

Foreword

The Long Corridor at St. Patrick's College in Maynooth, Ireland's last seminary, is slightly foreboding. The dark halls are lined with pious portraits of the clerics who, since 1795, have educated more than 11,000 Roman Catholic priests. Under the gaze of painted saints and angels on the ceiling, the College Chapel's marble mosaic floor looks like something out of Heaven. Outside, there are three Gothic buildings which comprise St. Mary's Square, overlooking a lush, green garden, and a pond with rock positioned like stepping stones, designed to symbolize man's spiritual journey toward God.

On a crisp, sunny morning in October 2004, I walked these grounds with Shane O'Doherty, through a stone archway into a Gothic quadrangle called St. Joseph's Square. We walked along gravel paths that snaked through grassy swaths bathed in bright red flowers. The only sound was that of the birds.

The last time we had gone for a long walk together, a decade earlier, in Shane's hometown of Derry, I was covering the conflict in Northern Ireland for The Boston Globe and Shane was a married man six years removed from prison. Before his arrest, he was the most wanted man in Britain, a hero for the Irish Republican Army because he had carried out a letter-bomb campaign that maimed a dozen people and terrorized millions of others. As we walked through Derry, we paused at the rooming house for British soldiers where he had planted his first bomb in 1970, when he was 15 years old. We passed the spot in the Bogside where Barney McGuigan's brains spilled onto the pavement on Bloody Sunday in 1972, when British paratroopers shot and killed 14 civil rights demonstrators. We walked by the apartment in Crawford Square that Shane had used as a bomb factory, the one that blew up, killing Ethel Lynch, his 22-year-old assistant.

He was given his middle name because he was born on the Feast of the Conversion of St. Paul, who was a terrorist and a murderer before he walked to Damascus. Shane's story is not about a miraculous, religious conversion as much as a gradual, spiritual evolution. He had a tug of war with God, and God won. His odyssey, from teenage revolutionary to a prisoner of nearly 15 years to middle-age seminarian back to ordinary Irishman is a story of redemption.

"Hell," he says, shrugging. "If I can be saved, anyone can. In 1965, when he was 10 years old, Shane tore a sheath of paper from loose-leaf notebook he used to copy lessons at school and wrote this pledge: "When I grow up, I, Shane Paul O'Doherty, want to fight and, if necessary, die for Ireland's freedom."

Even at his tender age, he knew his words were seditious, because he lived in a corner of Ireland still under British rule, and so he hid them, under the floorboards in the attic of his family's home, and forgot about them until ten years later, when he was sitting in an interrogation room, and a detective shoved the yellowed paper under his nose. He blushed, more embarrassed by his childish idealism than terrified at the prospect of spending the rest of his life in prison.

Shane was born in Derry, in 1955, during a winter so cold his mother called him the Snow Baby. Unlike Northern Ireland as a whole, Derry had a Catholic majority, and an established Catholic middle class, one of the reasons the Catholic civil rights movement bloomed there in the late 1960s. Shane was part of that middle class, one of eight kids in a family that wasn't especially political. His father was a teacher and principal at a Catholic school run by the Christian Brothers. His mother hailed from a prominent business family. Two of his uncles fought the British in Ireland's war of independence in the 1920s. But Shane's father never spoke of any of this and quietly aspired to unity with the Irish Republic while opposing violence as a means of achieving it. Despite holding the majority in Derry, Catholics were excluded from exercising power in a normal democracy through gerrymandering and other discriminatory practices of the Protestant unionist government that was loyal to Britain. London looked the other way, until 1969.

Most of the O'Dohertys' neighbors were Protestant, and Shane grew up never hearing a sectarian word at his dinner table. But as a child, he sat alone in his family's well-stocked library, reading about Irish history.

"There was something about the tragedy of British rule in Ireland, against the wishes of the Irish people," he says.

He was spellbound reading about the Easter Rising of 1916, when a quixotic band of patriots staged a rebellion they knew was doomed. It was a blood sacrifice, meant to fail, to trick the British into overreacting, and of course the Brits did. They always did, when it came to Ireland. If the Irish never forgot their history, sometimes to their detriment, the British never remembered theirs, invariably to their detriment.

As a 10-year-old, Shane O'Doherty offered himself up to martyrdom, which was something of an empty pledge, not because of his age, but because at the time, there was no rebellion. The IRA, widely regarded as a small, impotent bunch of dreamers with a handful of rusty guns, was dormant.

But that all changed when the Protestant unionist government's response to the demands of the Catholic civil rights movement was to beat protesters off the streets. In 1968 and 1969, around the time Shane was entering adolescence and should have been chasing girls, he began chasing IRA recruiters. Derry convulsed with protest and attacks on demonstrators by loyalist mobs and the predominantly Protestant police force. By the time British troops were deployed, ostensibly to keep the peace, Shane had thrown a Molotov cocktail at police and the IRA had become active again. A new group, the Provisional IRA, or the Provos, had sprung up, determined to bring the fight to the British, and 15-year-old Shane O'Doherty began an almost farcical search for them, knocking on doors, so he could join. He eventually found two men who inducted him into the secret, illegal organization.

"I was no longer an insignificant teenager," he said. "I became heroic overnight. I felt almost drunk with power."

At 16, he threw nail bombs at British soldiers and almost hoped he'd be shot dead, fantasizing that his blood sacrifice, like that of the martyrs of the Easter Rising, would inspire a mural, or better yet, a song, ensuring his immortality. He jumped out of alleys, firing a primitive, six-shot revolver at soldiers armed with automatic rifles. In 1971, he fired a rocket at a British Army observation tower. It missed, but hit another army post by dumb luck. Soldiers opened fire on a passing car, wounding an innocent woman and two children. Shane went home and prayed that the woman and her children would survive. They did, but his having unwittingly almost caused their deaths shook him. He stopped reporting for duty.

Any chance he would stay away from the IRA for good evaporated five days after his 17th birthday, when British paratroopers opened fire on Irish demonstrators on the streets of his hometown, on January 30, 1972, on what became known as Bloody Sunday. He saw unarmed men and boys gunned down. In the chaos, he bumped into a priest he knew and the two of them went to the local morgue, where police and soldiers laughed and joked about the shootings and the victims. He accompanied the priest to the homes of the dead and the injured, and his fury smoldered. He reported back to the IRA, and was flattered when his commander asked him to go to London to launch a letter bomb campaign.

"I had come to the conclusion that all these British soldiers from working-class backgrounds that we were shooting and blowing up in Northern Ireland were deemed expendable by the British government," he says. "The idea was to have those in high places in British military and political circles face the consequences of occupying Ireland."

Once in London, he posed as a student and bought a copy of "Who's Who," to draw up a target list. One of his bombs injured Reginald Maudling, the British cabinet member in charge of security on Bloody Sunday. He sent a bomb to Bishop Gerard Tickle, the Roman Catholic chaplain to the British Army, after reading a newspaper story quoting Tickle as saying British soldiers did nothing wrong on Bloody Sunday. He later learned the story was not true. The bomb, stuffed into a hollowed out Bible, failed to detonate. He sent a letter bomb to 10 Downing St., the Prime Minister's residence, and it sat unnoticed in a wastebasket for 24 hours. It didn't explode, but Shane's ability to pierce security at the very heart of the British government made him, as the mystery letter bomber, the most wanted man in Britain.

Other bombs exploded at the London Stock Exchange, the Bank of England and a British government building. The injured included secretaries and security guards, and, as a result, self-doubt returned. He went back to Derry and knelt in a confessional at St. Eugene's Cathedral, where he had been a choirboy a few years and a whole lifetime before. He told the priest he was in the IRA and wanted to talk about the morality of violence. But the priest was in no mood to debate liberation theology.

"Murder and violence are always wrong," the priest told him.

Shane, still just 19, left that church a more tormented than when he entered.

In 1975, the IRA called a ceasefire, with the promise from authorities that IRA operatives would not be arrested as a political compromise was hashed out. But that turned out to be an empty promise, and in May 1975 police descended on Shane's mother's house. His mother, who had no idea he was in the IRA, was making lunch and watched in silent bewilderment as her son was bundled into a car, shirtless, and whisked away by the Special Branch.

The IRA shot a police officer in retaliation for Shane's arrest. The dead cop was the son of the chief prison officer where Shane was being held, and the guards beat Shane mercilessly the next day. Guards ripped sheets into long strips and placed them in his cell, advising him to hang himself because it would be better than what they had in store for him. One guard sat outside his cell and turned the light on and off, so he couldn't sleep. Years later, the warden who presided over his torture was shot by the IRA, and Shane was ashamed of himself because, no matter how much he tried, he could not muster sympathy for the murdered man.

Shane was regularly tossed into solitary confinement as he refused to conform with prison rules. He read books about the theory of just war. He was trying to justify his own use of violence. But as he prepared for his trial, he read the reports that chronicled in clinical but shocking detail the extent of the injuries he had inflicted on 12 people. A secretary was blinded by glass in her eyes. A security guard had his hand blown off and an eye blown out. Another man lost the tips of his fingers.

Even as Shane second-guessed himself, he remained defiant before the Crown. He refused to recognize the authority of the court that tried him in London. The feeling was somewhat mutual, as the elderly judge who presided at his trial frequently nodded off. The judge woke up long enough to give Shane 30 life sentences.

If St. Paul's conversion was on the road to Damascus, Shane's was in solitary confinement in Wormwood Scrubs, the London prison where he was first incarcerated. His conversion was in the monastic tradition of Ireland, where monks preserved European civilization during the Dark Ages. Where guards saw only a stubborn man who refused to wear prison clothing, insisting he was a political prisoner who should not be treated like a common criminal, Rev. Gerry Ennis, who served as the Catholic chaplain at the prison, saw someone struggling to come to grips with his past.

"Your little brother is an extraordinary young man, given very special gifts, and I believe those gifts are going to be used for the greater glory of God," Ennis wrote in a prescient letter to Shane's brother in 1977. "I have never worried particularly about his being in the (solitary) Block, because he was always a person who was searching for the truth. Once the discovery was made, his prison cell became a monastic cell where he was alone with God and his own thoughts."

Shane emerged from solitary, still defiant toward a prison regime he saw as needlessly cruel to inmates, but he was changed. At tremendous personal risk, he left the security of the IRA cellblock, associating with English prisoners at a time when the Irish in England were held collectively responsible for the IRA's use of sometimes indiscriminate violence.

Back in his cell, he began reading the Bible more closely, more reflectively. The Gospel of Matthew nagged at him, especially one passage:

> So, if you are offering your gift at the altar, and there
> remember that your brother has something against
> you, leave your gift there before the altar and go; first
> be reconciled to your brother, and then come and offer
> your gift.

"I had rejected the Church's Doctrine of a Just War," he says. "I had come to believe that only pacifism was truly moral, truly Christlike. But, as

I was trying to make myself a better person, to distance myself from the violence I had committed, I couldn't really move forward until I had addressed my victims."

Shane then did what no other IRA volunteer had ever done: he apologized to his victims. He never heard back from them, though one, a security guard who lost an eye and hand, told British newspapers he opposed the prospect of Shane being released from prison. Shane didn't expect or need to be forgiven. The point was his being able to apologize and admit he was wrong.

In 1985, after a decade of protest, demanding his repatriation, Shane got into a taxi with two guards for the drive to Birmingham airport, for the short flight to Belfast. One of the guards handed him a religious paperback. The guard said he and his wife had been praying for Shane for months. Having grown up with a reflexive hatred of what England had done to Ireland, after ten years of being tortured, physically and psychologically, in English jails, Shane left the country with tears in his eyes because of an Englishman's unsolicited kindness.

Upon his release in 1989, Shane enrolled at Trinity College in Dublin to pursue a degree in English. A few years later, he met a pretty blonde from Chicago named Michelle Sweeney who was studying for a doctorate in medieval history at Trinity. They married, settling into a small house in Dublin. He got a job as a software trainer. As he prospered in Ireland's booming high-tech economy, he tried to soothe a troubled conscience. He edited a weekly magazine sold by the homeless. He volunteered to help Bosnian Muslim refugees. He taught computer skills to children from itinerant families.

Mickey, as Michelle is known, accepted an offer to teach in the United States, but Shane could not get a visa to live in the US because of his conviction for his actions on behalf of the IRA. In the late 1990s, even as other former IRA members who never expressed remorse for violence they'd committed flitted in and out of the US, promoting the peace process, Shane was repeatedly turned down permission to enter. Shane had been ahead of his time, and it cost him. By swearing off violence years before his erstwhile comrades in arms did, he became persona non grata with the IRA and Sinn Fein, its political wing. Sinn Fein decided who would be given the okay for visas to the US, all of it rubberstamped by a US administration wedded to the peace process, and the Shinners weren't about to reward someone they did not consider a team player.

It is a great irony that Shane's early repudiation of violence led to his marriage becoming a casualty of the peace process.

In the spring of 2001, Shane was sitting at his desk in Stockholm, where he was working for a mobile phone maker. He was just a former – a former terrorist, former prisoner, former husband. He had a good salary, and he was miserable. He went back to Dublin. In just a generation, Ireland had gone from being one of Europe's poorest countries to one of its richest. But the sudden, widespread pursuit of materialism disturbed Shane. It nagged at him, as his conscience had nagged at him in prison, as he took an account of his youthful idealism.

The priesthood intrigued him, even as a kid. But if his record precluded him from getting into the US, how could he possibly get into a seminary?

On a religious retreat, a priest sidled up to him and asked him if he had ever been on a retreat before.

"Yes," Shane said.

"How long was it?" the priest asked.

"Fourteen and a half years," Shane replied.

Like his marriage, the priesthood thing didn't pan out the way he envisioned. But those are stories for another day. There are, no doubt, other books in Shane O'Doherty. But this is the first one, about growing up in the belly of the beast, in Derry, where the Troubles of the latter half of the 20th century began, and where they ended for Shane O'Doherty.

This is a book about one man's dalliance with extreme nationalism – actually one boy's dalliance – and it demonstrates all too well how the glorification of violence, institutional discrimination, bigotry and the failure of democracy can produce extremists even in the comfortable middle class.

How Shane came out the other side of all this, a whole, compassionate, thoughtful, and not unflawed human being is a story of redemption, of spiritual awakening, of honest reflection.

It is not an Irish story. It is a human story. And it is Shane's story.

Kevin Cullen
Boston, Massachusetts
July 2008

CHAPTER 1

Forever A Usurpation

"When I grow up, I want to fight and, if necessary,
die for Ireland's freedom.
Signed: *Shane Paul O'Doherty*."

I was ten years old when I wrote those words on a page torn from a school exercise book. I hid the paper underneath a floorboard in the attic of my home in Derry, Northern Ireland, and promptly forgot about it. It was not posterity which discovered the buried note almost ten years later, but the Royal Ulster Constabulary searching my home while I was on the run and an explosives' officer in the IRA. A detective showed the faded document to me during my interrogation and commented that he'd never come across anything like it. I was surprised and embarrassed by my childish passion laid bare in its innocent cursive script. Despite a lawyer's efforts to have this property returned to me, it languishes still in an R.U.C. file in a police station, too seditious to be freed...

I had no doubt even as a ten-year-old that I would one day be a volunteer in the IRA fighting to end the age-old injustice of the British occupation of Ireland. There was nothing I wanted more from life and it seemed to me the most heroic and patriotic service I could render my country. What brought me to that youthful point of view, and to the later teenage realization of it? What ultimately changed my mind about IRA violence, about all violence, whether British or Irish, Protestant or Catholic? I shall try to explain the forces and events which helped to shape the course of my life, beginning with the very first one – my birth.

Procreation is like revolution – there is nothing democratic about it. So, like the Irish Republic, I was born bloody and surprised, kicking and screaming. It wasn't so bad that I was born as the seventh child to the wife of a schoolmaster, with, already, four brothers and two sisters for company, nor that my birthday, the 25th of January, was so cold that for years my mother referred to me as "the snow baby".

No, it was that I was born in Derry City, Northern Ireland, in 1955, to a Roman Catholic, Irish Nationalist family, thirteen years before the outbreak of the Civil Rights' Movement and fourteen years before the IRA began yet another campaign to drive the British out of Ireland. I was set up. In retrospect the snow was an augur of inclement times to come in my life.

It would certainly have caused a frisson in the palpitating hearts ofmy happy mother cradling her newborn baby, and my father celebrating the problem-free birth, if they had foreseen that their child, at the age of thirteen, would experience in the Civil Rights' era fierce riots in the Bogside and, a year later, the arrival of the British Army on the streets of Northern Ireland; that, at fifteen, he would join the Official IRA's youth wing and, almost immediately thereafter, transfer to where the real action was, the Provisional IRA; that, at sixteen, he would see the effects of internment without trial on Derry families, meanwhile taking part in bombings and shootings as often as the IRA would allow; that, at seventeen, he would be so close to the rifle-firing British paratroopers on Bloody Sunday that the friend with whom he would be running would be captured by them; that, at eighteen, he would send letter bombs to prominent British personages, bomb London, and, at twenty, would be treacherously arrested by the Royal Ulster Constabulary during an IRA ceasefire; that, finally, at twenty-one, he would be sentenced by Lord Justice Thesiger at the Old Bailey in London to thirty life sentences and twenty years in prison.

No, there is nothing democratic about procreation. The child, for his part, must not merely accept his parents as they are, warts and all, but also the historical time and place into which they introduce him. He must suffer the nationality and religion, culture and names which are foisted upon him. He must become a player in a costume and on a stage pre-ordained for him. Whoever created the whole going forth and multiplying scheme left a great deal to be desired.

My Roman Catholic parents, blissfully ignorant of my future, named me "Shane Paul" – the latter in honor of the Feast of the Conversion of St.

Paul the Apostle on which I happened to be born. A relative who registered my birth felt that the child of a father whose surname was Doherty and a mother whose maiden name had also been Doherty should bear the more Irish and more fitting clan-name of *O'Doherty*. She duly registered the birth of one Shane Paul O'Doherty, little realizing how often Roman Catholic schools would request to see the birth certificate of the child whose surname differed (by its first letter) from that of his "father".

Not merely was the name problematic, but the nationality too – because I was born in the disputed territory of Northern Ireland, which the Republic of Ireland claims and Britain occupies, I could be either British or Irish, or, if I so wished, have dual citizenship. Thus was I born, named, and nationalized twice over – and without any say whatever in such vital matters.

I was born in two places simultaneously: Roman Catholic/Irish Nationalist people call Derry *Derry*, while Protestant Unionist (i.e. pro-British) people call it *Londonderry*, and that's official. So even the name of the city of my birth was problematic, as it still is today.

Derry was a bad place to be born. Although it was a majority Catholic and Nationalist city, it was controlled by the Protestant Unionist minority by gerrymander, the unfair redrawing and manipulation of electoral boundaries. That situation was not going to last forever and I was born in time for the bloody change. Catholics either rotted in Derry without work or emigrated to find it elsewhere, so it is not surprising that my four brothers and one of my sisters left Derry while I was still quite young; my younger brother left while I was in prison; I am the only male of the family in Northern Ireland now. (Two of my brothers became American citizens.)

On removing me from the City and County Infirmary where my bum was slapped to evoke the first of my many protests, my parents did not have to travel far to reach home. We lived in the long downhill sweep of the wide road immediately below the hospital, Clarendon Street.

Clarendon Street and its large, Georgian red-brick houses were then almost an integral part of the hospital. Some houses had been joined inside to form large nurses' homes and a surprisingly large number of doctors and dentists (and their families) lived in the others and even practiced from the ground floor or basement surgeries. The street also sported a chiropodist, a denture-maker, Clarendon Springs on top of which Madden's Mineral Waters' business flourished, a huge Young Women's Christian Association Hostel, music and Irish Dancing teachers and quiet houses discreetly offering full board, or, less respectably, bed and breakfast. Nearly every house bore one or more brass plates which maids (some in uniform) carefully polished with Brasso each morning, nodding or waving to each other as they did so. At the City Centre end of the street, a shirt factory (Derry was famous for its shirt factories), a betting office and an Italian fish and chip shop "lowered the tone" considerably.

The area ministered not merely to the flesh, but also to the soul: there were at least five churches of different denominations in the vicinity, including the huge and imposing St. Eugene's Cathedral where I was a choirboy for some years. Sundays saw parades of conflicting religion, all of them sprung from Jesus Christ, but few reflecting his love.

Those whom religion failed might seek refuge in the somewhat chilling Municipal Lunatic Asylum set in its own spacious grounds behind a huge, long wall in adjacent Asylum Road. In retrospect, many of the politicians and churchmen later to deface Northern Ireland might usefully have been confined there, but their futures, like my own, were hidden. Instead, the new police headquarters was fittingly built there.

The Lough Swilly Bus Company was based a street away and ferried Derry holidaymakers to Donegal and back all summer; it also carried hundreds of Catholic girls to and from the rural Thornhill College every day, a fact which came to interest me considerably as I grew older. Other large shirt factories were nearby and so every day waves of women and girls, patients and penitents, flowed through the street more regularly than the tides. It was a busy area and I came to find the working women and girls, and the largely unemployed men and boys, the norm.

Behind Lower Clarendon Street and the commercial Strand Road was the wide and sluggish River Foyle, port and lough dividing Northern Ireland from Donegal in the Irish Republic. It sported an American Naval Base and many visiting navies and sailors from ships and submarines. It was natural to be attracted to the quays in the evenings to stand alongside docked subs, whose sailors threw coins and notes to the gazing children – "Give that to your sister!" they cried as the notes landed coin-laden at our feet. At eight or nine years of age, I couldn't figure out how they knew we had sisters or why they wanted to send notes to them at all. I fought all the time with one of my sisters – surely they wouldn't want to write to her!

But Clarendon Street was very respectable and quite well-off; it was fairly snobby and inhabited by Protestant and Catholic professional and business people (mostly Protestant) among whom, I always felt, my moderately-off family was a little out of place. Most families in the street owned at least one car, some two, and others kept speed-boats in their garages which they raced on Lough Foyle at weekends. Ours apart, most houses had one or more maids or housekeepers to look after the children (or the bachelor doctors), and special playrooms for the kids. Well-off families, Protestant and Catholic, tended to send their children to boarding schools. We were not that wealthy.

My father, who taught for decades in the Brow of the Hill Christian Brothers' Primary School overlooking the Bogside, hadn't owned a car since his marriage. For years he had the character either to pedal a bicycle to and from school or to walk the long distance in all weathers, his winter protection being a huge, heavy trench coat, galoshes and sturdy umbrella.

Two of my father's brothers, William and George, took part in the Irish War of Independence. George O'Doherty later became a Lieutenant-Colonel in the Irish Army, while William became a civil servant. Both lived in Dublin. The only reference I ever read in print about my father's family's involvement in the Old IRA (a term used to describe the IRA during the Irish War of Independence from 1918-21) was in an issue of "The Capuchin Annual" for, appropriately, 1969. It noted that the Doherty home in Waterloo Street had been an IRA contact-house during the War of Independence. I did not discover this fact until I was active in the IRA and "on the run". The veteran Derry Old IRA survivor, Neil Gillespie, told me in his home in the Brandywell in the early 1970s that my uncle George saved him from summary execution when he was captured as an Anti-Treaty Irregular by the pro-Treaty IRA. My aunt Lizzie played her part in the Old IRA as well, as her collection of medals proves. Unfortunately, I never sought to hear her experiences, a fact I came to regret too late when she died.

I never met my uncles George or William and my parents' contact with the Dublin end of the family was very infrequent, being restricted to occasions of weddings and funerals. Dublin was always a long way from Derry in more ways than one, as it still is. If I ever heard my father mentioning George or William, I must have paid scant attention. He never spoke a single word to me about his family's involvement in the Old IRA or about those times, nor did he ever utter in my hearing a single comment for or against Republicanism. I almost never discussed politics with him or ever heard him state any strong party political viewpoint. He was just another of those silent supporters of Eddie McAteer's Nationalist Party until, I suppose, the advent of the Social Democratic and Labour Party, latterly led by John Hume, when he'd have become an equally silent supporter of the SDLP.

So, my father devoted himself to his wife and family and to his teaching. He died in May 1973 at the age of sixty-five, a month before he was to retire as Principal of the Brow of the Hill school and when I was eighteen years old. If he had lived, I have no idea how he would have taken my arrest in '75 and my subsequent Old Bailey trial for London letter bombings. I do know how he reacted to the discovery of my involvement with the IRA, about which more later.

Unlike my father, my mother, Sarah, came from a well-to-do family of business people. Her parents left their native Inishowen, Donegal, in 1910 and moved to Greenock in Scotland where my grandfather set up a marine store and had scrap metal interests. The onset of World War 1 four years later brought him financial gains. My mother and her two elder brothers were born in Greenock and, in 1916, while she was an infant in arms, her parents returned to Donegal.

My grandfather, John Doherty, set up his marine store in Derry and started a bus service between Derry and Donegal. In 1926 he moved to

Derry and the scrap metal merchant's business he founded still operates today under his name.

My mother attended Thornhill College on the outskirts of Derry and, when she finished school, completed a course in hair styling and beauty culture and set up her own salon. A couple of years later she met my father at, of all places, an Eye, Ear and Throat Hospital Ball in Derry Guildhall. They married in July 1939 and – typical of their timing – honeymooned in Holland, Belgium and France where hoteliers pointed out the war preparations all around. My grandparents lived next door to us in Clarendon Street along with my aunt, her husband (who was Scots) and her family.

I grew into boyhood in the shadows of two sisters and was aware that four elder brothers existed beyond them, but I had little to do with the latter until I was much older. For four years I was the baby of the family until an eighth and final child arrived, whereupon I escaped the mollycoddling due to the "wee wean" of a family in Derry.

The elder of my sisters, Brenda, was very loving and motherly towards me and I often went to her for cuddles and comforting when my mother scolded me, or when I wanted extra affection. The younger one, Moira, who was less than two years older than I, was always in competition with me and hostilities continued for years. When I was a child just getting used to sleeping in a bedroom by myself, she often crept to the open bedroom door (which let in salvific light from the landing) and, before slamming it, shouted "The Bogeyman's comin' tae git ye!" ...As the door slammed, the overpowering darkness closed in upon me, bringing terrors with it, and I lay in sweaty paralysis until I could muster the courage to leap out of bed and dash across the dark room in the general direction of the door handle, which darling Moira sometimes held fast from the outside!

Each bedroom in our large house had a fireplace and a chimney and these were eventually decoratively boarded up. At night, and particularly in windy weather, particles of brick and plaster sometimes rattled down the chimney and hit the board, causing me panic and a virtual heart attack! Even without a sister or a noise to frighten me, the crush of theological and mythological facts and fancies I was learning had turned the bedroom darkness into an arena where ogres, bogeymen, devils and angels might appear and terrify me.

I was taught to fear God because He might send me to Hell to burn in a pool of everlasting fire. I was told that I had an eternal soul inside me which could be disfigured by venial and mortal sins, or else shone clean by an act of contrition or sacramental confession. I thought my soul was a silver plate inside my belly which was shiny bright when I was good and on which black marks appeared when I was bad. Worst of all, I was introduced to death as a horrible occasion of Judgment and tussling between an evil devil and a good angel for my soul. Death might at any moment snatch me away from my family and from the home and happiness I enjoyed, and not all my tears or crying would prevent it. Death was, I knew, the interruption of the heartbeat. Picture me, therefore, as a child in a dark bedroom cowering under the blankets, paralyzed with dread lest the noises coming from the chimney or wardrobe or window were the devil's tricks, wondering if Death were about to pluck me from Life and if my racing heartbeat were a prelude to an infant heart attack!

I vividly remember one night when the terror became too much for me and I fought my way free of the constricting blankets, floundered through the dark to the door, hoping against hope that neither devils nor ghosts would waylay me! I raced downstairs in time with my racing heartbeat and opened the dining-room door to my mother and father and shouted "Mammy! Daddy! I think I'm dying!" The light and heat and normality of the room already made me feel silly. My parents laughed at my fears, commented that I was an "oul feardie" and ordered me to find my own way back to bed, finishing with some comment about me being a nuisance. In high dudgeon, I complained, "Well, I didn't born me!" My parents' surprised reaction to this unexpected repartee has made me remember it down the years.

Of course, I didn't have to guess where babies came from – I *knew*. God created babies out of nothing. In fact, He made the babies appear in incubators on the top floors of hospitals – nearest to heaven – and the nurses lifted them up and brought them to the parents. God just kept on making the babies appear in the hospitals and the nurses kept on giving them to parents who wanted them – parents went to hospital to get them, didn't they?

After bedtime, I often took to sitting on the stair-carpet in my pajamas as close to the ground floor as possible without being visible to anyone in the hall; that way I felt close to the heat and light and company I missed. I would sit on the stairs in a sleepy state until I heard someone else coming up to bed, when I'd scamper up to my bedroom and take comfort from that someone's proximity. I got to know which stairs creaked or groaned when stood on, a knowledge which much later proved useful to me when I wanted to sneak silently out of the house at night.

While I was still the baby of the family, I was already benefitting from the attentions of our next-door Protestant neighbors, the Buchanans. Their ageing housekeeper, Mrs. Colhoun, regularly delighted me with beautifully wrapped birthday and Christmas presents. On these occasions, she would be supported by Scott Buchanan, the son, and their handsome wire-haired terrier, Pickles, would make a tremendous fuss of me. They were the kindest neighbors you could wish for.

Directly across from us lived the Moores, a Protestant business family who owned a large furnishings' shop in the city centre. As an infant, I played with their youngest son, Terence, on and off for some years. The Moores often drove to a seaside resort, Castlerock, at weekends and frequently took with them Aodh O'Donnell, son of less well-off Catholic neighbors, as playmate to Terence.

Relations between Protestants and Catholics in the area were friendly and extremely courteous. I never heard an ill word spoken at home about our Protestant neighbors; indeed, it would have been difficult to find in any of them any ills to complain about since they were mostly so respectable and good living. In later years, I was not surprised when my two sisters married sons of Protestant business families and when one of my brothers married the daughter of another Derry Protestant family. Even after I became involved with the IRA, I, too, courted a Protestant girl for a time before I went "on the run".

However, I wasn't the only child in the area who felt a crush of theological or mythological facts and fancies as the following recollection shows: I sometimes played with a child called Scully who lived in a side street off Clarendon Street. His mother was a widow who lived somewhat as a recluse and kept her children indoors with her as much as possible. She had a few Corgi dogs (in imitation of the Queen, everyone said) and was a Protestant. When young Scully and I were barely five years old, our happy playing together was bruised by religious tenets which obviously came from an adult. He one day said to me in a sly, fascinated manner "You're a Roman Catholic! You worship the Virgin Mary and you're going to Hell!" It was not the content of the remarks which hurt me, since I hardly understood it any more than he did, but the rejection implicit in it which came right out of the blue.

I never forgot this minor hurt for the simple reason that it was the single occasion of religious intolerance I experienced in my childhood. I knew it originated with an adult because I had only recently experienced a different type of intolerance, this time from the Catholic mother of the very best friend of my childhood, Raymond.

Raymond was the son of a successful Catholic doctor and lived next door to the Scullys. We were introduced when we were still infants and remained inseparable until the 11-plus examination caused our ways to diverge. (I passed the dreaded exam and went to St. Columb's College grammar school in Derry; he failed and was sent off to a boarding school).

The issue that caused his mother to object in my hearing to her son's association with me was a stutter which dogged me in childhood. I used to stutter when excited or when in the presence of strangers. My stutter affected only the first word I intended to speak, not the others that followed it, but I sometimes had real trouble uttering that first precious word; if I could get that first word out, the rest would come easily. I hated going to shops because my stutter would usually cause me an agony of embarrassment in front of strangers (or girls). I preferred to carry notes which spoke for themselves.

Raymond's mother a number of times complained to her husband that Raymond might "catch" my stutter if he were allowed to continue playing with me and her complaints were aired in front of me as if I were too young to comprehend the rejection at work in the adult words. The doctor must have put his wife right, because Raymond and I were "best friends" for years and my crucifying stutter had all but disappeared when I went to grammar school. The rare remnants of it struck others as a kind of Bertie Wooster-like affectation, a "snobby" manner of hesitating before choosing my words – if only they'd known...

The arrival on the scene of my new young brother changed my life. The youngest child of a Catholic family in Northern Ireland may be known by the colloquial diminutive "wee wean", but he or she is destined to be the focus of parental attention, particularly when the older children are preparing to leave home. Fergal released me from all that, and I found myself, paradoxically, in his shadow, a niche all the more secured by the fact that my elder sisters took the remaining attention. I exploited this relative freedom and invisibility as I grew older, taking advantage of the size of the house and the availability of upper floors and rooms where I might play undisturbed for hours. Given my responsible guardian angel role over Fergal and my relatively inconspicuous position, it was always assumed that I was doing the right thing wherever I was.

I rocked this assumption once or twice, though not deliberately. The worst possible accident occurred to put me in the spotlight for some months – I had the usual penchant for, among other boyish weapons, slingshots, or catapults, and spent many a happy hour becoming expert in their use. One day as I played with Raymond outside my home, I saw my cousin Michael walking down the other side of the street. I put an apple core in my slingshot and fired it up into the air intending it to land in front of him – to my lasting amazement and horror, the apple core not only came down on the sloping windscreen of a "bubble car" parked beside him – but shattered the glass as well...

Raymond and I hid in my house, going to the front room from where we could view what I may be allowed to call the burst bubble car. I watched in increasing terror as a bespectacled lady approached the car, examined the windscreen and was promptly met by the young daughter of a doctor neighbor, who spoke to the lady and pointed at my house. The lady crossed the street, and rang our doorbell, holding the informer by the hand... My mother answered the door and my name was called – in a grey, sick funk, I went to my doom.

"Shane, did you shatter this lady's bubble car windscreen with a slingshot?"

"Yes." I meant to add that it was an accident, that it was not intended, but my stutter prevented me. Anyway, the fact that the windscreen was shattered and that a slingshot had been used implied that it was indeed deliberate. I entered a period of shame and disgrace, compounded by the fact that the replacement of the windscreen cost the then relatively huge sum of £5. I was not allowed to forget this £5 worth of mischief and had to earn my way into the good books by dint of cleaning, scrubbing and generally being an angel around the house, which I eventually managed.

My only previous experience of lawbreaking had been a shattering encounter with two armed members of the Royal Ulster Constabulary on board a Lough Swilly bus parked in Clarendon Street one Sunday. My friends, Protestant and Catholic, and I managed to get into the bus and were playing happily in the seats – there was no question of damaging anything, by the way – when two armed constables came on board and got us by the ears to scold us. We cried our eyes out there and then. (R.U.C. constables were always armed and in those days wore massive holsters containing huge Webley revolvers.) The constables threatened to tell our parents about our misbehavior, and then let us go.

I didn't really know much about the political or cultural differences underlying the friendships I took for granted in the street. Sure, one or two kids were not so willing to talk to Catholics, obviously because their families trained them not to. But the same inclinations could be found in some Catholics not wanting to play with other Catholics.

However, when a new family moved into the Clarendon Street area, the "sausage Dohertys", so called because their father ran a successful butcher's business, the differences emerged slowly but surely. The Sausage Dohertys were a Catholic family whose father had a prominent role in the

Nationalist Party. The three elder sons, Seamus, Ian and Tucker, all older than I, not to mention the girls, Máire and Evelyn, took over the street games we played. I recall many occasions when Tucker debated with Derek, a Protestant friend from an adjoining street, the "link with Britain" as the British occupation of Northern Ireland was euphemistically termed.

Derek's main argument was always that Britain saved Ireland from invasion by Hitler's hordes. Tucker's reply was that being invaded by Britain's hordes hadn't been a boon to Ireland in the first place... Derek would then reply with the advantages of the British-underwritten health and social security network over the poorer Republic of Ireland economy and so the debate would go on, but it occurred in an entirely friendly manner. For the first decade of my life, street friends were categorized according to character or personality, not religion or politics.

As I began to read and learn more about the world around me, I would felt a slight passion thrill in me that we Irish Catholics had a cause, the cause of seeing Ireland united and the British occupation and border removed for ever. But it was no more than a childish passion. On the great Protestant and Orange annual day, July 12th, when the Protestant planters literally paraded their victory and superiority over the defeated native Catholics, I was once or twice taken by my brothers to the bottom of Clarendon Street in the early 1960s to view marchers and bunting and flags. There was, to my childish eyes, nothing about it but a festival in summer sunshine. I do recall my father saying to my brothers, "Don't be going down there!" – the implication being that Catholics were either not safe there or should not, for reasons of basic pride and principle, go there at all. My brothers might have had in mind that it was a mark of some bravado to be at an Orange parade however temporarily, or else that no-one was going to keep them indoors in their own area – I am not sure which. I do remember that they kept me prominently displayed while they were there.

But the first actual fear I ever felt about being a Roman Catholic occurred when I was about eight or nine years old, when the conversation was full of the news that a Protestant rabble-rousing preacher called Ian Paisley was coming to Derry. I vividly remember playing on the street with

Raymond and saying to him, "Catholics are going to be attacked – we are going to be burned out of our homes!" Paisley was to my childish mind the first ogre I encountered outside a tale, and I always associated him with the evil threat I felt as a child.

I had heard of the IRA, but there was something about it I couldn't quite understand – I could never figure out how anyone managed to join the IRA if it was a truly secret organization! How did you go about finding the IRA if all the IRA members were secret? I puzzled over this for a long time and still hadn't figured it out when I first sought to join the IRA at the age of fifteen in 1970. Did someone in the IRA keep an eye out for possible recruits, and if so, what sort of signals should one send out in order to attract the secret watcher's attention? One might go a whole lifetime sending out the most sincere signals and yet remain completely undiscovered! This was the riddle of my childhood, which troubled my sense of logic for many years.

My attraction to the IRA was not initially based on the sight or experience of any particular social injustice, though, when I did join the IRA, injustices were foremost in my motivation. It was the discovery of the tragedies of Irish history which first caused my desire to give myself to the IRA, and the best part of that history I imbibed alone at home reading books I found in the family library. It was the pure political injustice and tragedy of British rule in Ireland against the wishes of the Irish people which fired my anger, not forgetting the Famine and mass emigration.

The Irish history which thrilled me began on Easter Monday, April 24th, 1916 when Patrick Pearse read the following document to a curious crowd outside the General Post Office building in O'Connell Street, Dublin, at 12.45pm:

THE PROVISIONAL GOVERNMENT
OF THE
IRISH REPUBLIC
TO THE PEOPLE OF IRELAND

IRISHMEN AND IRISHWOMEN: In the name of God and of the dead generations from which she receives her old tradition of nationhood, Ireland, through us, summons her children to her flag and strikes for her freedom.

Having organized her manhood through her secret revolutionary organization, the Irish Republican Brotherhood, and through her open military organizations, the Irish Volunteers and the Irish Citizen Army, having patiently perfected her discipline, having resolutely waited for the right moment to reveal itself, she now seizes that moment, and supported by her exiled children in America and by gallant allies in Europe, but relying in the first on her own strength, she strikes in full confidence of victory.

We declare the right of the people of Ireland to the ownership of Ireland and to the unfettered control of Irish destinies, to be sovereign and indefeasible. The long usurpation of that right by a foreign people and government has not extinguished the right, nor can it ever be extinguished except by the destruction of the Irish people. In every generation the Irish people have asserted their right to national freedom and sovereignty; six times during the past three hundred years they have asserted it in arms. Standing on that fundamental right and again asserting it in arms in the face of the world, we hereby proclaim the Irish Republic as a Sovereign Independent State, and we pledge our lives and the lives of our comrades in arms to the cause of its freedom, of its welfare and of its exaltation among the nations.

The Irish Republic is entitled to, and hereby claims, the allegiance of every Irishman and Irishwoman. The Republic guarantees religious and civil liberty, equal rights and equal opportunities to all its citizens, and declares its resolve to pursue the happiness and prosperity of the whole nation and of all its parts, cherishing all the children of the nation equally, and oblivious of the differences carefully fostered by an alien Government, which have divided a minority from the majority in the past.

Until our arms have brought the opportune moment for the establishment of a permanent National Government, representative of the whole people of Ireland and elected by the suffrages of all her men and women, the Provisional Government, hereby constituted, will administer the civil and military affairs of the Republic in trust for the people.

We place the cause of the Irish Republic under the protection of the Most High God, Whose blessing we invoke upon our arms, and we pray that no one who serves that cause will dishonor it by cowardice, inhumanity, or rapine. In this supreme hour the Irish nation must, by its valor and discipline, and by the readiness of its children to sacrifice themselves for the common good, prove itself worthy of the august destiny to which it is called.

Signed on behalf of the Provisional Government:

THOMAS J. CLARKE, SEAN MAC DIARMADA, THOMAS MACDONAGH, P.H. PEARSE, EAMONN CEANNT, JAMES CONNOLLY, JOSEPH PLUNKETT.

The Proclamation of the Republic announced the Rising of Easter Week, a short-lived armed insurrection by a fairly small number of men who occupied certain buildings in Dublin and waited to be attacked and overcome by superior British forces, which is exactly what happened within a matter of days. Sixteen leaders of the Rising were executed by the British, and many others, including Eamonn de Valera, were imprisoned. Within a short time, this patriotic self-sacrifice, or the British execution of the leaders following hasty courts martial, gave rise to the War of Independence in Ireland which the IRA fought and partially won. Twenty-six of the thirty-two counties of Ireland were won back from the British by the IRA, but six stayed under British rule, and became called Northern Ireland.

Certain writings, poems and last words of these executed patriots and of others who had gone before them were collected and printed under various titles such as "Speeches From The Dock" (the one I first read) or

"Last Words". These writings ignited in me a passionate patriotism and an equally passionate desire to emulate the heroic deeds recounted therein.

The following are a few examples which captured my imagination when I began to read them at home when I was only nine years old. (Picture me, therefore, sitting crying in the large, curio-filled attic of my home, reliving the sacrificial combats of the heroes...) Commandant-General Pearse, President of the Provisional Government, managed to convey a few writings out of the besieged G.P.O. building before it was destroyed by British bombardment, among them a manifesto on 28th April, which read:

"The Forces of the Irish Republic, which was proclaimed in Dublin, on Easter Monday, 24th April, have been in possession of the central part of the Capital, since 12 noon on that day. Up to yesterday afternoon Headquarters was in touch with all the main outlying positions, and, despite furious, and almost continuous assaults by the British Forces all those positions were then still being held, and the Commandants in charge were confident of their ability to hold them for a long time.

During the course of yesterday afternoon, and evening, the enemy succeeded in cutting our communications with our other positions in the city, and Headquarters is today isolated.

The enemy has burnt down whole blocks of houses apparently with the object of giving themselves a clear field for the play of Artillery and Field guns against us. We have been bombarded during the evening and night, by Shrapnel and Machine Gun fire, but without material damage to our position, which is of great strength.

We are busy completing arrangements for the final defense of Head-quarters, and are determined to hold it while the buildings last. I desire now, lest I may not have an opportunity later, to pay homage to the gallantry of the Soldiers of Irish Freedom who have during the past four days, been writing with fire and steel the most glorious chapter in the later history of Ireland. Justice can never be done to their heroism, to their discipline, to their gay and unconquerable spirit, in the midst of peril and death.

Let me, who have led them into this, speak, in my own, and in my fellow-commanders' names and in the name of Ireland present and to come, their praise, and ask those who come after them to remember them.

For four days they have fought and toiled almost without cessation, almost without sleep, and in the intervals of fighting they have sung songs of the freedom of Ireland. No man has complained, no man has asked "Why?" Each individual has spent himself, happy to pour out his strength for Ireland and for freedom. If they do not win this fight, they will at least have deserved to win it. But win it they will, although they may win it in death. Already they have won a great thing. They have redeemed Dublin from many shames, and made her name splendid among the names of Cities.

If I were to mention names of individuals, my list would be a long one.

I will name only that of Commandant General James Connolly, Commanding the Dublin division. He lies wounded, but is still the guiding brain of our resistance.

If we accomplish no more than we have accomplished, I am satisfied that we have saved Ireland's honor. I am satisfied that we should have accomplished more, that we should have accomplished the task of enthroning, as well as proclaiming, the Irish Republic as a Sovereign State, had our arrangements for a simultaneous rising of the whole country, with a combined plan as sound as the Dublin plan has been proved to be, been allowed to go through on Easter Sunday. Of the fatal countermanding order which prevented these plans from being carried out, I shall not speak further. Both Eoin MacNeill and we have acted in the best interests of Ireland.

For my part, as to anything I have done in this, I am not afraid to face either the judgment of God, or the judgment of posterity."

Pearse was a poet too and among his last poems was the following, scribbled before his execution but not discovered until 1965 when Leon O'Broin found it among the Asquith papers in the Bodleian Library, Oxford. It shows the distinctly religious and sacrificial nature of the patriotism burning in Pearse:

A MOTHER SPEAKS
Dear Mary, that didst see thy first-born Son
Go forth to die amid the scorn of men
For whom He died,
Receive my first-born son into thy arms,
Who also hath gone out to die for men,
And keep him by thee till I come to him.
Dear Mary, I have shared thy sorrow,
And soon shall share thy joy.

The following is an extract from Pearse's address to his Court Martial:

"When I was a child of ten I went down on my bare knees by my bed-side one night and promised God that I should devote my life to an effort to free my country. I have kept that promise. As a boy and as a man I have worked for Irish freedom, first among all earthly things. I have helped to organize, to arm, to train, and to discipline my fellow countrymen to the sole end that, when the time came, they might fight for Irish freedom. The time, as it seemed to me, did come, and we went into the fight. I am glad we did. We seem to have lost. We have not lost. To refuse to fight would have been to lose; to fight is to win. We have kept faith with the past, and handed on a tradition to the future....I assume that I am speaking to Englishmen, who value their freedom and who profess to be fighting for the freedom of Belgium and Serbia. Believe that we, too, love freedom and desire it. To us it is more desirable than anything in the world. If you strike us down now, we shall rise again and renew the fight. You cannot conquer Ireland. You cannot extinguish the Irish passion for freedom. If our deed has not been sufficient to win freedom, then our children will win it by a better deed."

Thomas MacDonagh, another of the signatories who was facing execution, if he actually made the whole of the following address to his Court Martial – and it has been attributed to him regardless, even becoming the subject of a sedition court case – was prophetic:

"I choose to think you have but done your duty, according to your lights, in sentencing me to death. I thank you for your courtesy. It would not be seemly for me to go to my doom without trying to express, however inadequately, my sense of the high honor I enjoy in being one of those predestined to die in this generation for the cause of Irish Freedom. You will, perhaps, understand this sentiment, for it is one to which an Imperial poet of a bygone age bore immortal testimony: "Tis sweet and glorious to die for one's country..."

You would all be proud to die for Britain, your Imperial patron, and I am proud and happy to die for Ireland, my glorious Fatherland... There is not much left to say. The Proclamation of the Irish Republic has been adduced in evidence against me as one of the Signatories; you think it already a dead and buried letter, but it lives, it lives. From minds alight with Ireland's vivid intellect it sprang, in hearts aflame with Ireland's mighty love it was conceived. Such documents do not die.

The British occupation of Ireland has never for more than 100 years been compelled to confront in the field of fight a Rising so formidable as that which overwhelming forces have for the moment succeeded in quelling. This Rising did not result from accidental circumstances. It came in due recurrent season as the necessary outcome of forces that are ever at work. The fierce pulsation of resurgent pride that disclaims servitude may one day cease to throb in the heart of Ireland – but the heart of Ireland will that day be dead.

While Ireland lives, the brains and brawn of her manhood will strive to destroy the last vestige of British rule in her territory. In this ceaseless struggle there will be, as there has been, and must be, an alternate ebb and flow. But let England make no mistake. The generous high-bred youth of Ireland will never fail to answer the call we pass on to them – will never fail to blaze forth in the red rage of war to win their country's Freedom. Take me away, and let my blood bedew the sacred soil of Ireland. I die in the certainty that once more the seed will fructify."

James Connolly, Commandant-General of the Dublin Division and in command at the General Post Office, was twice wounded, the second time seriously, by British Army snipers during the fighting, but carried on. Captured, weak from loss of blood and "not improving", he was nevertheless propped up in bed for the Court Martial and later propped in a chair for his execution. His address to his Court Martial was:

"We went out to break the connection between this country and the British Empire, and to establish an Irish Republic. We believe that the call we then issued to the people of Ireland was a nobler call, in a holier cause, than any call issued to them during this war, having any connection with the war. We succeeded in proving that Irishmen are ready to die endeavoring to win for Ireland those national rights which the British Government has been asking them to die to win for Belgium. As long as that remains the case, the cause of Irish freedom is safe.

Believing that the British Government has no right in Ireland, never had any right in Ireland, and never can have any right in Ireland, the presence, in any one generation of Irishmen, of even a respectable minority, ready to die to affirm that truth, makes that Government forever a usurpation and a crime against human progress.

I personally thank God that I have lived to see the day when thousands of Irish men and boys, and hundreds of Irish women and girls, were ready to affirm that truth, and to attest it with their lives if need be."

If writings such as these were not enough to fire my youthful blood and idealism and to fill my eyes with tears – and believe me, they were – then the records of the Franciscan Capuchin priests who attended the patriots before their executions certainly did so. To take just one of many poignant examples, writing of the execution of Major John MacBride, who had fought in the Irish Brigade against the British in the Boer War, 1899-1900, Father Augustine, O.F.M. Cap., recalled:

"After two o'clock this morning a loud knocking was heard at the Bowe Street gate [of the monastery]. I went down and a soldier told me I had been asked for by one of the prisoners at Kilmainham. I was prepared, owing to information received the previous evening at the Officer's quarters on the North Circular Road, and went at once.

On reaching the prison I was immediately shown to a cell and on its being opened I gripped the hand of Major MacBride. He was quiet and natural as ever. His very first words expressed sorrow for the surrender, and then he went on quickly to say that on his asking for water to have a wash a soldier had brought him a cupful. "I suppose," he added with a smile, "they think I could wash myself with that much." He then emptied his pockets of whatever silver and coppers he had and asked me to give it to the poor. Finally, placing his Rosary tenderly in my hand, he uttered a little sentence that thrilled me: "And give that to my mother."

Then, having given me a message for another that convinced me he was a man of very deep faith, he began his Confession with the simplicity and humility of a child. After a few minutes I gave him Holy Communion and we spent some while together in prayer. I told him I would be with him to the last and that I would anoint him when he fell. When the time was up a soldier knocked at the door and we went down together to the passage where final preparations were made. (I seem to see it all now vividly again, and as I write I feel naturally stirred.) He asked quietly not to have his hands bound and promised to remain perfectly still.

"Sorry, Sir," the soldier answered, "but these are orders." Then he requested not to be blindfolded, and a similar answer was given. Turning slightly aside, he said to me, quite naturally, in a soft voice: "You know, Father Augustine, I've often looked down their guns before."

Later a piece of white paper is pinned above his heart, and, inspired by the Holy spirit, I whisper into his ear: "We are all sinners. Offer up your life for any faults or sins of the past." And this brave man, fearless of death, responds like a child, yet firmly: "I'm glad you told me that, Father. I will." The two soldiers and myself now move along the corridor, turn to the left and enter a yard where the firing squad of twelve is already waiting with loaded rifles. Six now kneel on one knee and behind them six stand. He faces them about fifty feet from the guns, two or three feet from the wall. The two soldiers withdraw to the left, near the Governor and the Doctor, and I, oblivious of all but him, stand close at his right, in prayer. The officer approaches, takes me gently by the arm and leads me to a position below himself at the right. He speaks a word. The prisoner stiffens and expands his chest. Then quickly, a silent signal, a loud volley, and the body collapses in a heap. I moved forward quickly and anointed him, feeling the meaning of the beautiful words of the Liturgy as, I think, I never felt them before, and the certainty of the consoling thought that the soul of the dear one who had fallen was already on its way to God and His Blessed Mother."

At the age of nine and ten I very definitely was engaged in lonely and emotional communion with the spirit of these writings – meaning that I cried my eyes out while reading them – to the extent I wrote and hid my own Pearsian note already described. I might often write with a vein of irony or satire, but it would be untrue to play down the patriotic dedication that I felt for years before there was any outlet for it, and the absolute confidence that I would be involved in an IRA campaign.

It was all very well to have the right predispositions to put on the costume of an IRA hero or martyr and take part in Ireland's freedom struggle, but Ireland was without a freedom struggle at that particular moment. Fate however was well on its way to providing one, and the first big signs I noticed of its coming appeared in 1966 when I was eleven and already a first year student at St. Columb's College grammar school in Derry.

The IRA's most recent struggle then, such as it was, had begun in 1956 in what came to be known as "the Border Campaign" (which quickly fizzled out and was declared defunct by the IRA in 1962.)

A decade later, in 1966, the Irish Republic celebrated the 50th anniversary of the 1916 Easter Rising with an impressive show of appreciation, nostalgia and a "march past" at the General Post Office building in central Dublin watched by Irish Government ministers and visiting delegates. As an eleven-year-old grammar school student, I watched the celebrations with interest.

Not wishing to be totally left out of the celebrations, the IRA blew up that oppressive remnant of British occupation, Nelson's pillar, in central Dublin and caused a rush for the shattered bits – so many people claimed to have chunks of it, that, had the pieces been reassembled, Dublin Corporation would have been able to raise three columns in place of the original. However, it was a stunt to catch the imagination of the nation, particularly that part of it living in public houses. Coming after gregarious, drinking Brendan Behan, who married the mystique of the IRA and his imprisonment to writing – his bestselling novel, "Borstal Boy", and his plays, "The Quare Fellow", "The Hostage", etc. – it was a time when Ireland could indulge the IRA somewhat because it was almost totally inactive and a threat only to ugly phallic symbols of British colonial architecture. A rise in the popularity of Irish traditional and folksy music, much of which paid tribute in song to IRA heroes and martyrs, added to the IRA's absent acceptability. I thrilled to the explosion in Dublin.

Finally, for my purposes, the pro-British and Protestant Ulster Volunteer Force paramilitary organization shot dead two Roman Catholics in Belfast in 1966 – Peter Ward and John Patrick Scullion – indicating that the bottom line of Northern Ireland life for Catholics was that, apart from being discriminated against in jobs and in housing allocation, and apart from being brought up to emigrate, you could be shot dead as an enemy of Ulster by sectarian bigots with guns. They had the guns, but, if we hadn't any, we had the new nostalgia for the IRA, and that was going to prove lethal enough. The UVF was to explode the first bombs in Northern Ireland a short time later in protest at the Northern Ireland Prime Minister seeking better relations with the Republic of Ireland and considering granting reforms to Catholics.

The first signs of social unrest in Derry that I remember were associated with an issue that, paradoxically, mobilized Protestant and Catholic alike, and which focused on the location of Northern Ireland's new second university, (the first being Queen's University in Belfast.)

I am going to simplify the tale: Derry, Northern Ireland's second city with a Catholic and Nationalist majority, was controlled in every respect by the Protestant and Unionist minority through a shameless gerrymander almost fifty years old. You might imagine that this control would sometimes have worked to the advantage of the city, since the Protestant and Unionist persons controlling it lived there and were rearing their children in it, but you would be wrong. A group of the most influential, who came to be called "the faceless men", worked against the interests of Derry in order to prevent any change of political control, to prevent the building or allocation of houses which might go to Catholics, and to prevent a university being sited in a majority Catholic city. They succeeded too. The New University of Ulster, as it was named, was sited not in Derry, but in a Protestant Unionist market town called Coleraine, some thirty miles northeast of Derry.

It must be said that not every Protestant Unionist in Derry opposed the location of the university in Derry, and many Protestants were part of the furious protest which culminated in a famous "car cavalcade" to Northern Ireland's Stormont Parliament in 1966 when thousands of people protested at this most blatant discrimination against Derry City, but the protests were in vain.

It was very much a middle and upper-middle class protest – you had to have a car to take part in a car cavalcade and had to expect or desire your children to go to university – and it involved that rarely rebellious sector of society, the teachers, headmasters and parents. I remember it being discussed at home, and neighbors setting off in their cars to Stormont. I also remember the bitterness of the let-down.

Another more urgent protest was building up in Derry and other parts of Northern Ireland, which was primarily working-class and ghetto-based and which focused on the fundamental matter of the lack of housing for Catholics and the poor quality of what housing there was. This lit the fuse of street protest and of the Civil Rights Movement, which latter was destined not merely to oppose the armed forces of the Protestant Unionist Government of Northern Ireland with mass peaceful protest but to rock that unjust Government to its foundations. All in all, 1966 was a good year for the grapes of wrath, and a breakaway section of the dormant IRA – then not even dreamed of – was set to trample them.

Imbued, as I was, with the terrible beauty of the 1916 Rising, I did not think it impossible that another, and final, Rising might happen in Northern Ireland to finish British rule in Ireland once and for all, and, even at eleven years of age, I was certain that I wanted to be involved in the making of what I thought could only be a glorious final chapter in history. Little did I know that a terribly ugly offspring of that most terrible beauty was lurking just around the corner with arms outstretched to embrace me...

CHAPTER 2

Show Them Who's Master

By the end of 1968, I was already familiar with Civil Rights marches and the inevitable confrontations with the Protestant Royal Ulster Constabulary. These usually ended with police batons cracking Catholic heads, water-cannon soaking people, sometimes in indelible dye, and escalation into full-scale rioting in the streets, as on the most famous date of that year, October 5th.

On some occasions, when the Unionist Government banned all marches, Derry was the site of instant unscheduled and unstoppable street protests by either the dockers or the "factory girls" (the workers from the many shirt factories). It was astonishing to me that, in the space of a few months, what seemed to be the entire Catholic community of Derry – previously noteworthy for its soporific response to fifty years of injustice – united in public displays of protest such as mass "sit downs" in Guildhall Square. Nearly every Civil Rights demonstration was attended by a Protestant Unionist counter-demonstration, with the attendant armed police definitely on their side. The experience of sitting in defiant pacifist gesture among thousands of Catholics singing "We Shall Overcome" filled me with the belief that we were united in an almost mystical, religious unity and cause.

Since I lived in Clarendon Street beside the city centre, and near Victoria police barracks, I often started out behind the police lines among a crowd of Protestant opponents of the Civil Rights marchers, many of whom I either knew personally, or by sight, since they lived around me. During the mêlées, when lines of demarcation disappeared violently, I had to change sides quickly.

Clarendon Street was next-street-but-one to the focus of nearly all of the rioting for the next few years, the William Street/Rossville Street junction at the entrance to the Bogside, the defined Catholic ghetto. The Bogside was set to be the heartland of IRA activity. Unlike many of the people who lived in areas of the Bogside, Brandywell and Creggan, I and my family could hear the sounds of the rioting from home (which was so regular as to earn the local title of "the Saturday matinée"), including the shots of the police CS gas guns. We had often to sit tearfully indoors as the prevailing breeze brought the teargas in our direction and through our house.

My father had first taken me across the long Leckey Road – the artery of the Bogside – when I was about five years old to the prize-giving in his class at Christmastime. I distinctly remember the walk and his showing me off to the very many women and men who greeted him. In later years, being his son was a passport to being known and trusted. He and his sister, Mary, born and reared in Waterloo Street, had spent their lives teaching children in the ghetto. I walked the length of the Bogside four times every weekday after my eighth birthday, going to and from school in the Christian Brothers (where my father taught) and in St. Columb's College after that. I got to know the area intimately. The Bogside may have been only two streets from mine, but it was a totally different world.

To my young eyes, it was a strange, depressed place: dead and plucked chickens and geese hanging by their feet for sale in Rossville Street across from the cattle yard; herds of cattle, flocks of sheep, and some pigs being driven into the abattoir in the Little Diamond; horse-drawn carts carrying either coal or scrap iron; the mostly unemployed men standing idly at street corners talking, while others were walking groups of muzzled greyhounds on long leashes to exercise them for the Brandywell dog races; "winos" lying full-length on the footpath in drunken stupor or pestering people for their "odds"; tiny two-up-two-down houses built against each other all along Leckey Road with women every morning scrubbing the "front step", which included a small semi-circle of the footpath right at their front doors. When it rained, the Bogside had the biggest puddles I had ever seen, and since, as its name echoed, it had been an old river bed, it flooded with the greatest of ease. How people bore the constant flooding of their homes is beyond my ken.

I saw the Old Bogside being knocked down for redevelopment, and recall Morgan's rag-store collapsing and the hundreds of rats which fled it in all directions through clouds of dust as the horrified onlookers scattered before them... But I had lots of fun there. One day while we were walking to school, friends who were older than I told me to prepare for Anton Doot. "Anton Doot?" said I, genuinely puzzled. "Aye," they said, "and you better be able to run! See yer man wi' the lemon wisps of hair and the bulges in his jacket pockets?" they asked. "I do," I said.

The wee man was standing outside The Greyhound Bar at the edge of a group of men, with his thin, yellowing hair combed to cover his balding pate, but in vain. "Well then – ANTON DOOT IS A FRUIT! ANTON DOOT IS A FRUIT!" With that, they sped off and I turned to see why. Anton Doot was fumbling in his pockets and screaming in a thin voice, "Gone, ye wee fuckers yees! Yees wee fuckers!" He got half a house brick from his jacket pocket and proceeded to throw it with amazing strength after the leading runner, then pulled a second from his other pocket.

I could run alright, and I was speeding along in a thrill of real fear with my schoolbag bouncing against my back when the halved house brick tumbled along the road yards ahead of me. He had no more bricks. I stopped and turned to shout in my shaking voice, "Anton Doot is a fruit!" I was a manly, if quaking boy now, with one looming qualification: I couldn't go home past the enraged Anton after school and had to find an alternative route through St. Columb's Wells. And I didn't even know what a fruit was! We tortured Anton until we grew too sophisticated to run from any wee man and half-house bricks.

Everyone knew everyone else in the Bogside and Brandywell, and a stranger stood out like a sore thumb. The women conversed from their front doors about any stranger in the street, even in his hearing. I remember the first time my mother trusted me to call the chimney-sweep to our house; she gave me a written note to take to him in St. Columb's Wells, a tiny area of the Bogside outside and under the fortified walls of the city, where – obviously – there was a well linked by tradition to Columb himself, saintly founder of Derry. "How will I find his house, Mammy?" I asked her. "Don't worry, you'll find it," she replied casually.

My worry was that my stutter mightn't even allow me to ask anyone, but as I walked nervously around the little street, St. Columb's Wells, I needn't have troubled – small women at their equally small front doors asked me, "Who are you looking for, wee boy?" "The sweep," I replied triumphantly. This fact was passed up the street to the other door-watchers. "Who's your father?" "Master Doherty." "Och, that's Master Doherty's wee boy." I was in.

I had to give my age and other details, and was finally told where to find the sweep, who lived with his sister around the corner. I called and met the sooty, stertorous breather who did not know to wear a breathing mask, and handed him the note from my mother. He couldn't read the cursive script, and called his sister to the door. As they strained to decipher the note, I looked into the cramped, bare hall at the tiny staircase, and wondered how families of seven, eight, or more were reared in such confinement.

The sweep had a diction to be proud of, and, in a labored speech, said he'd attend the following day. I got to know him well over the years, and cleaned up after him at home, where his brushes and cloths failed to control the spread of soot, to my mother's considerable irritation. This sleepy St. Columb's Wells was to be attacked by a drunken mob of the Protestant Royal Ulster Constabulary in January 1969, as the Government-instigated Cameron Report was to state in paragraph 177:

"We have to record with regret that our investigations have led us to the unhesitating conclusion that on the night of 4-5 January, a number of policemen were guilty of misconduct which involved assault and battery, malicious damage to property in streets in the predominantly Catholic Bogside area, giving reasonable cause for apprehension of personal injury among other innocent inhabitants; and the use of provocative sectarian and political slogans. While we fully realize that the police had been working without adequate relief or rest for long hours and under great stress, we are afraid that not only do we find the allegations of misconduct substantial, but that for such conduct among members of a disciplined and well-led force there can be no acceptable justification or excuse."

However, in typical British style, no action was taken against the Royal Ulster Constabulary, which was the supposed guardian of the law, but was not constrained by any law where excesses against Catholics were concerned.

The event which had precipitated this police attack was the People's Democracy march from Belfast to Derry during the previous few days. Heroism in its various degrees, whether foolhardy or unsuccessful, British or Irish, always attracted me. Sitting at home listening to the television news at the end of 1968 and beginning of 1969, I heard about this small group of Civil Rights activists who were marching across Northern Ireland and who were being attacked along the way by groups of extremist Protestants who were sometimes actively helped to stage their ambushes by the police.

The vicious attacks on the passive marchers earned them a disproportionate amount of publicity, and people who formerly condemned their decision to stage the march at a time of great tension could not but react sympathetically. On the day that they were to arrive in Derry city, where a public meeting had been arranged in their honor in Guildhall square, it was a natural thought on my part to walk some miles out of the city to meet them. The walk took me (along with a school friend) through the predominantly Protestant east side of Derry, called "The Waterside". We met the marchers just beyond Altnagelvin hospital.

I can still remember my shock and fear on seeing them as they approached us. Bloodied and wearing makeshift bandages, they had been the object of a most brutal attack a few miles away at Burntollet Bridge by Protestant extremists. The watching police had stood by and done nothing to defend them, obviously condoning the attack. This was not new, but it was of immediate relevance that the route to Derry city centre meant going through a yet greater concentration of Protestant territory, with the possibility of further ambush. All of this was debated loudly and in something of a panic as we all marched along.

The concern turned out to be justified. The march was again attacked from high ground behind Spencer Road in the city close to Craigavon Bridge, and I remember bricks and bottles raining down on us as we ran along. Adults grabbed such teenagers as I and kept us in the sheltering lee of buildings over which the missiles were dropping.

My fourteenth birthday passed that month, while the situation in Northern Ireland deteriorated under the protests of the Civil Rights Movement and the violent counter-attacks of the police and their extremist Protestant supporters. Rioting became so commonplace that it was not unusual for a non-combatant to pick a path along the edge of a riot and through it to whatever business beckoned beyond it. Often on my way to or from school I melted around a riot and through a police line, it being obvious that I – wearing my school uniform – was not in that instance involved.

But the police were not to be relied upon to keep their batons off non-combatants. Two Catholic men, sixty-nine year old Frank McCloskey from Dungiven, outside Derry, and forty-two year old Samuel Devenney from William Street, died in 1969 as a result of attacks by the Royal Ulster Constabulary and no policeman was ever charged in connection with the murders. Sammy Devenney was attacked and batoned in his own home two streets from mine, a few doors from my aunt's house. Even the then Prime Minister of Northern Ireland, Major James Chichester-Clark, accused the Royal Ulster Constabulary of maintaining a "conspiracy of silence", but they kept the killers safely in their midst. They still hide murderers, as British policeman John Stalker's vain attempt to investigate RUC "shoot-to-kill" incidents in the 80s shows...

The mother of all battles which the police were at last to definitively lose was brewing for the summer of 1969. Summer is not really a happy-go-lucky time in Northern Ireland, but a period of Protestant pro-British marching to commemorate long-gone victories over the native Irish Catholics. The 12th of July is the day of the Orange parades (called "Orange" because of the marchers' allegiance to the Dutch William of Orange who was imported as Protestant Sovereign against Catholic James hundreds of years ago...) The Orangemen parade with loud bands and drums not merely in Protestant areas, but especially in Catholic areas – that's the whole point, to rub salt in age-old defeated Catholic wounds.

The 12th of August is the big Derry day, when the Protestant Apprentice Boys (Orangemen under a different name) parade through majority

Catholic Derry to commemorate the relief of Derry, which was under vain siege by forces loyal to Catholic James in 1690. The fact that all this was three hundred years ago is not the point either – it expresses the current balance of power very well, as seen by Protestant Unionists.

By August of 1969, Catholics in Derry were for having no triumphant Protestant salt-rubbing march through their area, while the many Protestant marchers from all over Northern Ireland were hell-bent on triumphalism, certain that the Protestant police would enforce their right to parade in a Catholic area. They were right and the stage was set.

I had been away for four weeks of Irish language summer school in Rannafast, Donegal, on a scholarship awarded for proficiency in speaking Irish. Rannafast is one of the Gaeltacht areas of Ireland, where Irish is still the first language. The four-week course included Irish dancing and singing with some emphasis on history, and, more importantly in my eyes, girls. Young people from all over Ireland go to these summer schools, and some come from abroad. Protestant children from the Republic of Ireland also attend. The executed patriot leader of the 1916 Rising, Patrick Pearse, had some early link with the foundation of the Gaeltacht school, which added to its appeal for me.

I distinctly remember on the last evening, during a Ceili dance at the college, going to a window to watch the setting sun with Máire Dempsey, a girl from Dublin whom I fancied. I gazed at the pink and red sky and said to her, "I wonder where we'll be in ten years." I already knew that the situation in Derry was so bad that the IRA had to come out from wherever it was, and I wanted more than anything in the world to be in its ranks. I had more than a premonition, a belief almost, that I would be either dead or in prison within a matter of years.

I got back home to find Derry more nervous than it had ever been in the wake of the police murders of the two Catholic men. Tens of thousands of people had attended the funeral of Sammy Devenney. The community was tense with the news that the infamous "B Specials" (an armed Protestant paramilitary force in support of the police) were on standby and were on the streets with rifles. The fact that thousands of Orange marchers were to parade on the edge of the Bogside posed a serious threat to Catholics living there and the television and radio news broadcasts were reporting these fears and calls on the Orangemen to call off their provocative parade.

The march went ahead and those parading little knew that this date would commemorate from then on not a victory, but the defeat of the Royal Ulster Constabulary and the arrival of British troops on the streets of Northern Ireland to maintain some semblance of law and order.

As the Orange march drummed its way past William Street, guarded by the Royal Ulster Constabulary, Catholics flung insults and stones. The police charged the Catholics and battle was joined – the Battle of Bogside, as it came to be called. When Royal Ulster Constabulary charged they ran into a barrage of stones and petrol bombs, and the fact that in their wake came a mob of Protestant Unionist bigots bent on attacking the Bogside only fuelled the fires. This began as the fiercest rioting I had ever seen. Petrol bombs rained down on police armored cars which had the temerity to drive into the ghetto. Rioters took petrol bombs right up to the police lines before throwing them. The battle raged through the night, with ground gained and lost on both sides. The police used CS gas in great quantities, without success.

Clarendon Street where I lived, and the adjoining one, Great James Street, became the battleground for a time. Barricades of post office vehicles (from a nearby garage) were placed across them to prevent police and Protestant mobs from attacking the Catholic cathedral. Blazing vehicles were sent careering down Great James Street towards the police and mobs when gunfire directed against us injured a number of people. I was at the top of Great James Street when two people standing feet from me were shot. I couldn't believe that my Protestant neighbors were massed at the bottom of the street from where the bullets were being fired. I also couldn't believe that we had no guns. I definitely thought that law and order were gone forever. Here were Catholics of all classes engaged in the violent defense of both the Cathedral and the ghetto, using every weapon short of guns – there were the Protestants and police firing bullets at us.

What could law mean from now on, when the guardians of it were the breakers of it?

I was tall and fast for my age – I was a cross-country runner at St. Columb's College. Added to this ability to outrun the police, I had a British forces' gas mask. (Far from being a product of a family of patriotic Irish bigots, I was quite used to British ways: my brother Cahir had just finished five years service in the British Royal Air Force and I prized the Services' watch he'd sent me from RAF Muharraq, Bahrain, for my birthday. My eldest brother, Eamonn, a teacher, was a member of the British Territorial Army for a time, and I purloined his gas mask from the wardrobe in his bedroom and took it to the front line of the rioting where the CS gas was concentrated. My first-cousin Raymond was also in the RAF.) The police were throwing rocks and stones, firing CS gas canisters at people, driving their armored cars at the crowd and pointing their weapons in a menacing manner.

I stood there watching until someone asked me to give up the mask to people on the roof of the highest block of flats in Rossville Street who were raining petrol bombs down on the police and making it impossible for them to enter the Bogside – this small group of fighters was disproportionately effective owing to the great height of the building. The police were firing CS gas grenades at them to no avail.

I gave up the mask, got a few deep breaths of CS gas into me and got over it after a bit. Everyone was breathing it and most were surviving it tolerably well with a variety of home-made remedies. These included handkerchiefs soaked in vinegar (which I found as bad as the gas) or barrels or buckets of water into which brave souls threw the hot canisters spewing gas. The fact was that I, in common with hundreds of other young people, could survive this stuff and still throw stones and petrol bombs.

My problem was that I was a virgin rioter – I hadn't actually ever thrown a petrol bomb. I watched with fascination the bravest of the brave who virtually ran up to the police lines before throwing their bombs, setting fire to "the black bastards" as the police were known from their uniforms. I saw that they were being supplied from a lane behind a wall right at the front line. I made my way to the lane and looked out at the fighters who were only yards from the armed police. Their courage amazed me and I instantly wanted to be one of them – they were singlehandedly stopping the police at the entrance to the Bogside.

I got a petrol bomb from a crate which was lying nearby and lit the cloth from someone else's device and – in an unforgettable mixture of calm and excitement – walked to the fore and beyond. I knew that I couldn't throw as far as the others, so I went beyond the foremost rioter. The police were stupidly massed at the corner and almost immobile, whether from fear of the ferocity of opposition or from tiredness I do not know. It was a simple matter to throw the petrol bomb right into their midst and watch them dance a scatter from the flames. It was an intoxicating power to exercise over a hated enemy and I wanted more. Above all, it taught me that I could do what I set out to do, that I could reach the forefront and beyond. I threw petrol bombs until I could throw no more. I thought this wasn't a bad initiation for a fourteen-year-old.

During the night, when the police with armored cars made a surprise charge along Infirmary Road above the cathedral, I and two other lads picked up a tall, heavy man who was lying almost unconscious from the effects of CS gas and we ran him up Creggan Hill out of reach of the police. As he regained consciousness, he thanked us profusely for saving him from capture and every time that I saw him thereafter he always thanked me, skinny kid that I was compared to him. It just went to show that size, weight and age were no barrier to usefulness during that period.

The worst experience I had during this rioting occurred in Rossville Street when the police fell back for the first time and seemed to disappear. In the garish light of burning buildings, the large crowd of Bogside defenders among whom I was standing and who had been growing more confident with every success, saw a mob of Protestants across in Great James Street, next to where I lived, who had been behind and supporting the police. I shall never forget the moment when a man near me began to shout, "Let's go and get them!" In that moment I visualized that it would be hand-to-hand fighting, bloody street war, right in front of my very eyes, involving Protestant and Catholic neighbors of mine, and I remember shouting, "No! Don't go over there! No!" I suddenly realized that I sounded like a panic-stricken youngster – which is exactly what I was – and I shut up and left the front line. For whatever reason, the direct confrontation between Protestant and Catholic did not happen in Derry.

Owing to the barricades and rioting, I could not get back to Clarendon Street at all, and had to stay out overnight. Hundreds of people stayed out around braziers all night ready to defend the neighborhood, and it was possible to get tea and sandwiches from local people. I was reporting back to my parents every day on the situation as I'd seen it from nearby streets, and I always gave the impression that I was merely an observer. Staying out all night was an exception, but was permissible only if the streets were too dangerous to negotiate. The earthquake in the political position of Catholics was so historic that exceptional rules sometimes applied.

Rumors of help from the Irish Government and Irish Army had been rife for some time, and the son of a well-known local leader was serving in the Irish Army and always seemed to be around, reporting – it was said – to Irish Army Intelligence the situation on the ground. I remember one rumor that Irish Army units were billeted in Celtic Park and another that they were poised at the Border, which was only a short distance from the Brandywell.

Everyone's worry was that, with this unprecedented victory over the Royal Ulster Constabulary, the police and B Specials would simply use live ammunition against stones and petrol bombs and the battle would be over. It was obvious that we had no guns – none had been fired in our defense in the area of the Cathedral when bullets had been fired at us. So, when a period of silence and calm descended in the wake of the police falling back for a time, it became ominous and everyone worried that they were getting ready to use guns. Some shots had been fired by the police during the rioting, but only in isolated instances.

There was very nearly celebration in the streets when reports circulated like lightning that the Irish Prime Minister, Jack Lynch, had stated on television that the Irish Government "would not stand idly by" while Catholics in Northern Ireland were subject to attack and siege. Here at last was some form of recognition from an Irish Republic which had stood idly by for fifty years while Irish Catholics in Northern Ireland were treated as second-class citizens. It seemed to confirm all the rumors that the Irish Army was poised to defend or rescue us if the police and B Specials attacked us with guns. I distinctly recall everyone saying that we just had to hang on, just had to keep the defensive fight going, that the Irish Army was going to move in to British-occupied Northern Ireland...

Then the British Army in their old-style steel helmets and cumbersome uniforms appeared and erected barbed-wire barriers across all the streets which the police and mobs had used to attack the Bogside. Instantly there was order, safety, security. Everyone was delighted that the British Army had put a ring of steel between us and the police and mobs. Everyone thought it historic that we had forced the British Army onto the streets of Northern Ireland by our victory over the hated police. The British Government, it was said, could no longer turn a blind eye to what was happening in Northern Ireland. I ran home to spread the news. I made sandwiches and coffee for the soldiers at the foot of Clarendon Street and Patrick Street and ran errands for them with money they gave me. I chatted with them for hours. They were not much older than I was. I did this for a few days and forgot completely about the earlier prospect of the Irish Army coming in. The heady perfume of the defeat of the Royal Ulster Constabulary was still strong in every nostril and we could be allowed a respite.

In my mind, I thanked the Orangemen for their march which had been the catalyst for this revolutionary victory. Sir Patrick Macrory, in his "Siege of Derry", recalls: "On the eve of the march in August 1969, I asked an Orangeman of my acquaintance, the kindest and most decent of men, why it was necessary to keep up these obviously provocative celebrations. He looked at me in mild surprise and then said grimly, 'We have to show them who's master, that's why.'"

But the mastery was now up for grabs and, for the first time in Northern Ireland, we Catholics had a slippery grip on it. We were so naïve. We wishfully thought that the British army was independent of our tribal

THE VOLUNTEER

battle, was English and fair, was peacekeeper... Fools, fools... The troops were being controlled by the very same rotten Unionist Government which controlled the police and B Specials.

It was noticeable within days. At the edge of the Bogside the army set up tents through which everyone coming or going had to pass, where there were tables and paper on which each person had to write his or her name, address and destination. This caused immediate anger. Why should not Derry people walk their own streets without having to write their details for the British army? What did the Army want this information for anyway? This information was not being collected in any other area. Collection of such information clearly showed that the British Army had quickly made up its mind that Catholics were subversives, were the dangerous section of the community. Far from defending the Bogside from police and mob attack, the British Army was sealing it off, not unlike the way that the spread of a disease was quarantined and controlled.

I and my friends made a point of going through these checkpoints as often as possible and arguing with the soldiers who were manning them. We wrote our names as Mickey Mouse and Donald Duck and gave fictitious addresses, and the soldiers didn't even notice. But I was angry, as were many more Catholics. I was all the angrier because only a few days before I had welcomed this army as a blessing defending Catholics from a sectarian Protestant Unionist police force gone berserk. From that moment, I lost any sense of welcome for the British Army and resented its presence on our streets.

The primary lesson I had learned during this fiercest rioting was that force or violence was something that everyone was prepared to use or condone as a last resort. The defense of the Bogside by violence was something which no-one in the community had criticized and in which everyone seemed to have played a part. Groups and committees had organized for it and had sought to gain credibility or prominence by alleging that they could exercise control over it. The Irish Government had hinted that it was prepared to use violence in support of us too. In Derry, the bravest of the brave and the local heroes were those who put themselves at considerable risk in the front line of violence. They were already being mythologized in tales and songs. I wanted to be one of the heroes and proficiency in violence was clearly a necessary qualification.

The news item which I regarded as most significant in 1969 was that the dormant and useless IRA organization had split in Belfast in response to the need to defend Catholic ghettos there by the use of guns. A graffito had appeared drawing the words "I RAN AWAY" from the letters "IRA" which was proof of Catholic dissatisfaction with the IRA when Catholic ghettos in Belfast had been attacked by police and extremist Protestant mobs.

The situation in Belfast, where Catholics were definitely in the minority, had gone beyond extreme, with streets of Catholic houses burned out by Protestant mobs seemingly aided by police, police firing mounted Browning machine guns into Catholic homes (in one incident killing a young boy asleep in bed), and a number of other Catholics wounded or shot dead. Many hundreds of people had fled their homes.

Stories were told of a handful of IRA men taking tremendous personal risks using some clapped-out guns and a small amount of ammunition to skillfully hold back better armed police and Protestant mobs, in some cases shooting attackers dead.

I was enchanted by the vision of these heroes putting their lives at risk to defend their people and by the news that they were forming a new Provisional IRA despite the great possibility of being involved in a bloody feud with the former parent body, now called the Official IRA. This new group, nicknamed "Provos", from the beginning was portrayed as an army prepared to use guns as and when necessary, and which, (unlike the Communistic Official IRA), was fervently Catholic, patriotic and aggressively defensive. I worshipped these heroes from afar. There could be no greater love than to lay down your life for your people or your country, I thought. At this stage I saw patriotism as laying down my life, not laying down anybody else's... It never occurred to me that the Protestant people had a cause or patriotism.

I now wrestled with my childhood riddle once more: if the IRA was a secret organization, and all its members were secret too, how could you ever find a way to tell it that you wanted to join it? There was no easy answer to this problem in Derry where the battle had been won without any IRA guns or bullets, with the result that there weren't any IRA men to be found.

I began to scour all the Republican publications I could lay my hands on for information or hints which might lead me to the IRA. I began to buy "The United Irishman" and saw the invitation to join Sinn Fein – you cut out a printed name and address section and mailed it to the Republican movement in Dublin, and a host of Special Branch and intelligence services garnered your details before the Republican movement received it in the mail... no thanks...

Eventually, after Easter, 1970, and in the wake of learning that I had missed a small Republican parade of uniformed persons in the Little Diamond a short distance from Clarendon Street, I decided to try my only option in Derry – to go to the published address of a Sinn Fein person in Creggan and state my real business if the opportunity offered. As far as I was aware there had been no news of any split in the IRA in Derry, so there should only be one organization if it existed at all.

So, feeling that History would hinge on this evening, that Patriots of previous campaigns were with me in spirit – because I meant to be heroically patriotic and famous like them as well – I set out on the relatively long, cold, dark walk up to Creggan. I wore my most manly clothes – I was fifteen and had every intention of saying that I was sixteen or seventeen.

I reached the nondescript terraced house and knocked on the door. No-one answered. I could tell that there were people in the house watching television. I knocked more loudly, but still no answer. I knocked even louder, too loudly. A man came to the door in some surprise. Before he could speak, I stuttered, "I've come about Sinn Fein." I held up a copy of The United Irishman. "I want to join."

He did not look like a Sinn Feiner at all. I was about to tell him that I really wanted to join the IRA, when he stunned me by asking a series of questions in an English accent. I answered them all, telling him my name, who my father was, where I lived, falsifying my age, but all the time I felt that here was a British agent! How the hell could somebody English be in Sinn Fein in Creggan, Derry, I wondered...

He went inside, and a younger, stockier, black-haired and intense man came out to me. He was a Derryman, with the look of a fanatic. I felt better about him. "You want to join Sinn Fein?" he asked. "No," I replied, "I really want to join the IRA." "Who's your father?" he asked. I told him. "I know your father," he said. "There's a meeting of some people this week – you come along and we'll talk about it." He told me where to go – it was a street called Thundering Down, near enough to Clarendon Street.

The conversation was over – he nearly smiled and shut the door. I set off home feeling both happy and dissatisfied. I had at least done something positive about my lifelong ambition, but what had I achieved? I was to go to a meeting with some people to talk – this was not what I had wanted to happen. I had wished for some recognition of my obvious potential, some celebration of my act of offering myself to The Cause, some sight of weapons or bombs, some immediate conferral of an impossible or fatal duty or responsibility to test me, but nothing of the sort had materialized. I was unhappy. I was impatient.

A few evenings later I went to the house in Thundering Down at the specified time and was admitted immediately by the intense, dark-haired man. I stepped straight into a small room where there were five or six other youths who obviously shared my desire to join the IRA. I was easily the youngest. I sat on the arm of a chair and waited.

A middle-aged man whom I had not seen before came in and stood in the doorway. He said, "Right then. You have all expressed an interest in becoming part of something larger. We'll see how you get on in a Militant Slua. ["Slua" is the Irish word for a group or unit]. Now I have to warn you what you are up against. When the Special Branch find out you are involved in this movement they will try to break you."

He stopped to let this sink in. He went on, "They will try to isolate you. They will even tell your parents and friends that you are a homosexual." He stopped, looking white and slightly ill. I was aghast... everyone else was aghast as well... This was not an honorable fight at all... I knew that I could fight for Ireland, die for Ireland, go to prison for Ireland, become a hero for Ireland, but to have to live under the allegation that I was a homosexual for Ireland – I didn't think I could... I was appalled... I felt sick... these Special Branch bastards would stop at nothing...

The room was grim now, and the patriotic, heroic effervescence had gone out of it completely. He continued, "Now you know what you are up against, and Donnelly is the Special Branch bastard you have to watch out for." He spoke with the grimness of someone whose family and friends had already been told by the police that he was a homosexual, and not a patriot or hero at all. He described the Branchman's car, giving us the registration as well, and told us where he lived. He told us to remain silent under questioning. I wondered why it was that he was so certain that we were going to become known to the police so fast. I thought we were supposed to be operating in secret, but I didn't want to ask a bolshie question of this pained individual.

"Now, you have to raise money for your Slua to finance your operations. If you pull in the money, we will get you the weapons. We will get you, for instance, a pen that emits gas."

I didn't think I was ever going to get so close to the armed enemy that I would be able to pull out a pen, press the button and knock him out with gas, but it was a beginning and I didn't know much about this sort of business anyway. It sounded sort of secret agentish and it could only get better. He suggested we rob some shops or businesses with our fingers poking in our pockets and made a point that arming was related to financing, and we were entirely responsible. This was not what I expected or wanted to hear, but it was a beginning. He declared the meeting over and told us to be back at the same time, same place a week later. He suggested we leave the house in pairs with some minutes between each exit and that we get to know our pair.

I got up thinking that this was not how the Sacred History books had implied it would all begin and looked at a tall, spotty-faced guy who looked back at me with similar feelings. We went out together and up the street.

"What do you think?" he asked me.

"It's not exactly what I expected," I replied. "Fingers, but no arms! Pens that fart! They never actually mentioned the IRA at all."

"It's not what I expected either, the bastard! Poke your fingers in your pocket! Poke them up his arse! Be better to go into a shop with a lit petrol bomb! Homosexuals my arse!" He was so angry that I felt I lacked an appropriate response. He introduced himself as Jim, and I told him my name.

"Is that your real name?" he asked. I said of course it was. He laughed and said, "Well, you start with the right name for a gunman, even if you have to poke your fingers!" For years, most people thought that "Shane" was a nickname. He knew another of the guys in the house, so we waited for him on Marlborough Terrace. I was introduced to him and he straightaway suggested robbing a number of shops during the next few days around the William Street area to speed the acquisition of weapons, preferably heavier than gas-pens.

The long and the short of it was that the following week, and for some weeks thereafter, sums of money were provided to this middle-aged man who merely gave us talks and promises of absurd weapons which in fact never materialized. The crunch came after two months or so of fruitless meetings and not a hint of weaponry or action. My friends said that they had called to the man's house in Creggan on two occasions and on the second visit noticed a new suite of furniture and a carpet. They thought the money we had supplied had been used to redecorate the man's house. I was furious and said I'd never again go back to the meetings. The others said they weren't sure it was a good idea to cut contact with this organization over one man who might be siphoning some money. I said that I was definitely not going back and that robbing small shops with my fingers poking through the material of my jacket was not how I wanted to fight for Ireland. (I may have omitted to mention earlier that I was a rash, hot-tempered youth, given to instant, irrevocable decisions.)

I did not go back, but I did regularly see the others who mentioned that my absence had been commented upon by the man who had tried to portray it as a possible security breach and who wanted to know where I might be found inside the ghetto. No-one had told him. I was angrier than ever. I told my friends that since the IRA had never been mentioned and since we had taken no oath of allegiance, no contract existed and I wasn't risking my freedom to redecorate anybody's house. For all that, I kept away from Thundering Down.

Meanwhile, I could see that History was hotting up, that there was a definite possibility of a Rising against British rule in Northern Ireland. It had just been announced on the news that two ministers of the Irish Republic's Government had been dismissed and then charged with conspiring to import arms destined for the Catholics of Northern Ireland. The former ministers were Charles Haughey (who later became Irish Prime Minister for thirteen years) and Neil Blaney, member for Donegal. An Irish Army Intelligence Officer, Captain James Kelly, had also been arrested and charged with the conspiracy. Another former minister in Jack Lynch's government, who had resigned in protest at the others' dismissal, was calling on Lynch to resign. It seemed that while Jack Lynch, the Irish Prime Minister, was indeed going to "stand idly by", others in high places weren't.

As I was walking across Rossville Street one day on my way to school, I met a childhood friend and another lad. Without any preamble, he said to me, with some bravado in his voice, "Do you want to join the Provos? We're going along to join tomorrow night." Stung by the fact that he had been able to find the Provos and I hadn't, and taken aback by his claim that they were "going along to join" the Provos as opposed to just talking about it, I said that of course I'd go along. They told me where to meet them and we parted. I walked on to St. Columb's College in some shock. I was troubled now by a feeling of anti-climax in having found the Provos – if indeed these really were the Provos – without actually finding them at all. My friend had found them, but how?

When my annoyance subsided, I discovered how a black hole in space might suck in everything around it, including light and time, because the prospective moment of joining the IRA was now the whole focus of my existence. Everything past, present and future, was focused into that point in time, everything bent toward it and I prayed to God above, "If I am to die, just let me live long enough to join the IRA – just let me join, then do with me what you will." I wanted time to speed up to the point where I could get on with joining in case something happened meantime to prevent me.

The following evening, feeling sure that this time the beatified spirits of Ireland's patriots were hovering close, I met the two others and set off. We went to a house in Waterloo Street where two men were waiting for us. I instantly saw that these two looked the part – intensity was everything. If they had a mind to encourage us to join the Provisional IRA, they hid it. The intensity of my feeling about that evening has enabled me to remember almost word for word what was said to us.

"If you have any doubts about joining the Provisional Irish Republican Army, then don't join. We are not promising you a pleasure trip. If you do join, then there is every likelihood that you will be imprisoned or killed within a short time. You have to know what you are getting into. Doubts are fine and you may leave with no hard feelings. We would prefer that you were honest with us and expressed your doubts or fears. This is a serious business. People will be imprisoned for a long time. Some will be killed. There will be no material rewards whatsoever, now or in the future. This is about armed force and freedom struggle against the oldest enemy of Ireland's freedom, an enemy which has never granted freedom willingly to any colony. We mean to fight for it and it will not be easy. You may leave now if you have any doubts whatsoever. Remember, that you will inevitably come into conflict with your families, girlfriends and friends. This is not an easy thing. We will leave the room for five minutes now and any one of you may go out with no hard feelings." They left the room.

I was in ecstasy – this was surely the real thing! Paul looked at me as excited as I was. "I suppose you're gonna leave, Shane?" "Yeah, after you," I joked. We waited in anticipation.

The two men came back looking every bit as serious as they had earlier. They asked two of us to go into the nearby kitchen and wait there. Paul and the other lad went out, leaving me.

"We are going to administer the oath of allegiance to you. If there are no witnesses apart from us, then the opportunity for someone to offer evidence in a court that he saw or heard you taking the oath will never arise, and so your chances of being convicted of membership of the IRA are diminished."

The importance of the moment and the solemnity these men attached to it made my heart beat faster. I could scarcely believe that I was about to become part of the Irish Republican Army, part of the heroic tradition of Ireland, but above all at that time, part of the defense of my people against the Royal Ulster Constabulary and its supporting mobs, and against the British Army. I was about to be on the inside of the Rising I believed was going to happen in Northern Ireland. God, just let me be a part of it, don't let it happen without me, even if I may only be a messenger boy, but let me be a part of it! I was also in line to be a martyr and hero among my people if I was killed in action, and I would achieve an immortality among the faithful remnant of the sacred tradition of Republicanism.

"Raise your right hand and repeat after me: I, Shane Paul O'Doherty, swear that I will strive to bring about the establishment of an all-Ireland Irish Republic according to the Army Orders of the Provisional Army Council and that I will obey all orders given to me by my superior officers, so help me God."

I said the words, barely aware of anything else owing to the pressure of emotion in me. The men had two others to "swear in", and were not to be expected to hang about while I soared in my ecstasy. I went to the kitchen and waited for the others to take the oath of allegiance. After their oaths were administered, we were given different times to call back to find out about the units we were to join. We left and I got away from my friends as soon as possible in order to be alone.

I walked home deliberately slowly so that I could savor the new existence I inhabited. Everything had changed utterly for me. Everything that I might do in the future, I would be doing for the IRA and for Ireland's freedom. I was no longer just plain insignificant teenage Shane Paul O'Doherty – I was a soldier, if a young one, of the Freedom Struggle, a secret member of the IRA which in the past had fought the Irish War of Independence to semi-success and which in the present was preparing to free Northern Ireland from British occupation. I had now the potential to become like the patriots with whose writings I had so often been in lonely communion and whose lives had had such a profound effect on the Irish nation. I was now a member of an organization which had conferred on me the potential to be like them. It only remained for me to be so assiduous in prosecuting my personal war that my superiors should have to notice my total dedication. In my mind on that walk home I was already far more advanced than a humble fifteen-year-old volunteer (who had in fact lied about his age); I was being shot dead in heroic circumstances; I was at the dock of the court making a defiant, fiery speech in the face of the might of British Injustice; girls cried over my sufferings and heroism...

In the days that followed I was seized by the most terrible temptation of my life. To an onlooker, it must have seemed that some pubertal or post-pubertal struggle was torturing me from within, but it was nothing hormonal. The temptation was related to the secrecy of my new, real self – I was above all supposed to keep my IRA membership secret, but a leak is always the shadow of a secret, or at least the temptation to leak. I already knew that I was special, but my excitement and pleasure and happiness about it were brimming over such that I thought I would burst if I did not tell someone. Then I was struck by guilt before the jury of my hovering patriots that I would want to prostitute the single efficacy I owned against the British, namely my anonymity, for a cheap thrill of recognition by another. I consoled myself with the thought that my anonymity would all the more cause people to react in a shocked manner when my true identity would one day become known – they would say, "Did he not grow up among us? And did we not think we knew him? And all the time he was a patriot!" So, that was to be my lot, to steal along in the shadow of a patriot!

But oh, the boredom of being a new IRA volunteer in 1970! It was excruciating... Because I had joined with two lads from the largely Protestant Waterside area across the river Foyle, I was firstly attached to a "section" there where the entire emphasis was on defense. There were the endless "parades" in our Section Leader's house, where we did little but learn to respond to marching commands given in Irish and where we stood at attention, turned on the spot and stood at ease. It was a long walk from my home in Clarendon Street to the outer reach of the Waterside and a longer walk home on a freezing, dark night, so I tried to suggest that I should be attached to a unit in the Bogside or Creggan near where I lived. Eventually, I was told I was to be transferred.

I was surprised to be transferred, because it would mean that I knew the details of two units, the one I'd left and the one to which I was now going, but I was not complaining. For some time to come, people in the Bogside took it for granted that I knew a lot more about the Waterside than I did.

The one fact that I had made known to help my transfer was my desire to work with explosives which put me in a category virtually by myself at that time. People who volunteered to work with explosives were regarded either as "nutty professors" or as stark, raving mad because explosives, commercial and home-made, were dangerous and unpredictable and had cost IRA persons their lives. In June 1970, a number of Derry Provos, Joe Coyle, Tommy Carlin and Tommy McCool had been killed in a premature explosion in Creggan. Two of Tommy McCool's children had also been killed. Result – not many people wanted to work with explosives.

If temptation leans on the bell, opportunity only rings once and I got lucky. Before I had anything other than a vague idea how bombs worked, I got one all to myself. Two senior Provos, who were trying to plant a bomb near where I lived, amazed me by arriving at my front door one evening. It was lucky that I answered the door to them, because they were older, mature men and I would have had difficulty explaining why they had called for me. They had a shoulder-bag with them which contained a bomb. They hadn't been able to plant it at the target and asked me if I could dump it somewhere until the target became more accessible.

I was excited and delighted by my good fortune. I was being given a look into the secret world of the IRA and its operations which would within a day or two grab the attention of the nation by exploding this very bomb. I asked them how the bomb worked and they told me that it was a very simple type which used safety fuse which, if ignited, would burn for three minutes before exploding the detonator and the bomb. They showed me the end of the safety fuse on which a number of matches were taped. Scrape a matchbox striker along the matches and they would flare, igniting the fuse, they said. To be safe, prevent the matches from igniting, and if they accidentally did so, cut the six feet of fuse or pull the detonator from the explosive. It all seemed pretty simple and clear to me.

I agreed to take the bomb and hide it somewhere, but not before I had extracted from them the target details. All of this – calling on me with the bomb, giving it to me to dump, telling me the target – was against the "need to know" rules of the organization, but these officers felt that necessity was the mother of *carte blanche*, and I was suddenly catapulted from simplistic ignorance of IRA activity, to active participation in it. I took the bomb somewhat gingerly and hid it in the loft of our back garage some distance from our house.

The senior IRA men intended me to dump the bomb until they or others could plant it. I intended to steal a march on them by planting it myself that very night. I only had to get the bomb to the target, strike a matchbox against the matches, wait for the fizz of sparks to verify that the fuse was lit, and then get away fast.

In the middle of the night, I sneaked downstairs from my bedroom and out to the garage where I lifted the bomb. I carried it over my shoulder through shadows and dark alleys to the target – the streets were completely deserted. My heart thumped loudly and painfully as I carried the bomb to the doorway of the target, and prepared to light the fuse. Would it blow up and kill me? Would I be caught getting away? Would I freeze from panic the moment I lit the fuse, like a rabbit blinded and paralyzed by the lights of a car, and be caught in the explosion?

All these panicky thoughts assaulted my mind, but I knew, if I wanted to be a patriot and hero, that this moment was make or break – anyone could hold a bomb or a gun, but only those who could look into the yawning jaws of danger and death and not flinch were going to make the grade. I put a matchbox against the matches and struck it along them. Nothing happened. All of me was shaking and I thought I would die from a heart attack. I struck again, the matches flared and there was an unmistakable fizz of sparks from the core of the fuse. It was lit! Go! Go!

I staggered away like a drunk person, shocked at my incredible pulse and trembling and made off into the shadows. I raced home. I even got upstairs to my room. There was what seemed like a small eternity of time. The fuse must have burned out!

As I wondered about misfires, an incredible roar and boom exploded over the entire city, magnified many times by the intense quiet of the night. Even from this distance, the sound of falling masonry and glass could be heard through the closed window. I went to my father's bedroom door. "Daddy, may I go and see where that was?" Just wakened from sleep, he said "Yes", and I leapt downstairs and out into the street. Other people were by now coming out from their homes and wandering around looking for the source of the blast, which was soon spotted via the debris on the footpath and road.

I walked to a corner with some neighbors and gazed along the street. A cloud of dust had been raised by the blast and it gave an eerie, misty quality to the sight which met my eyes. The building had been severely damaged, pieces of it were lying on the footpath and road for some distance, broken glass was everywhere and a number or alarm bells were ringing vainly against the awesome power which had been released. A man in nightclothes was running up the road some distance away, with his hands to his ears and screaming. He disappeared around a corner. A second man was picking his way over the debris, again in nightclothes, in a strangely staggering gait. Had they been in the building?

In the morning and all day, the media would report an IRA attack on a military target and would show the considerable damage on television and in press photographs. Everyone would think that an IRA unit had daringly breached security and planted a bomb. No-one would know that I, a fifteen-year-old volunteer, had done it by myself, without any real knowledge of explosives, without explicit instructions, without help and without difficulty.

I could not take it all in. There was supposed to be some preparation and training, some elapsed time, between not being an IRA bomber and becoming one – but everything had seemed to happen so quickly... I had not found the Provos myself, but had become one, and I had not become a bomber, but now was one – there was little or no transition period... I hadn't had time to catch up with my new self...

I walked home. The fact was that I was now an IRA bomber whether I liked it or not. I had crossed the one divide which was important to me and which I did realize – I was now linked to every patriot hero who had ever been executed by virtue of the fact that I had broken the law in a big way, had done an act which signaled my own being at war with Britain. I personally was at arms now, and the satisfaction grew within me with an increasing glow. From the time of my childhood when I dreamed of being an IRA hero to the present when I had joined and planted my first bomb, no effort seemed to have been required. It had all fallen into place for me. It seemed to me to have been fated.

Would the IRA officers think my attack was something to praise, or something to get me into big trouble? I had carried out an operation without explicit instructions, without their knowledge, and had cheekily exploded one of their bombs. I had taken a huge risk. How would they view me now? I would find out the next evening, and I grew more worried as I waited to report in. I was always inclined to break the rules first and consider the consequences only much later. Now I was considering the possible outcome and it could be good or it could be seriously bad. I waited to find out.

CHAPTER 3

My Patriotic Excess

My senior officers never imagined that a bomb they had put into safe keeping would, in the night and without their knowledge, wend its way to the target where they had failed to place it, explode there causing maximum damage, and, for the record, wake them in their beds. They certainly never expected a youthful, inexperienced and lone volunteer to carry out such an operation. Initially, they had been as mystified as everyone else in Derry about the source of the explosion, until they learned the target, whereupon suspicions began to dawn that I must have done it. However, they were in no position to suspect the years of prior dedication and lonely fantasizing which I had joined to my oath of allegiance.

When I reported to them, they questioned me in some detail about the bombing, implying that I had breached discipline and failed to understand the collective nature of the effort being organized by the IRA. When I admitted this, they relaxed a little, shook their heads in disbelief, laughed about it, and teased me over my cheeky eagerness to get into action. They were wary of volunteers who lacked an appropriate fear and respect for explosives and operations, regarding them as dangerous to everyone concerned, and would expel them from the organization. I seemed to satisfy them that while I was aware of the dangers involved in what I had done, I was nevertheless determined to operate.

In their minds, I had faced and overcome the considerable risks involved in transporting, planting and exploding the bomb at a military target in the middle of the night, and therefore I was an operator, not a talker. They took me seriously when I again asked to specialize in explosives, and they promised to arrange for me to meet and work with the best man they had in that field.

I had been catapulted into a minor prominence a year or two before I might otherwise have earned it, and it gave rise to another opportunity almost immediately. An operation had been suggested to bomb a government building, but no access point had been discovered. I was asked about my knowledge of the building, since I lived near it. I said I'd check it out, did so and found an entry point.

Since I'd found a way in and because I was familiar with the area, I got the job of actually planting the bomb and lighting the fuse. I was to wave from a window to another IRA person nearby to signal that I had ignited it, and this person would telephone the police and give a warning so that the building could be evacuated before the device exploded.

I was no expert on explosives or safety-fuse, but I did know that kinks, or sharp right-angle bends in the fuse wire, were likely to break the inner core of gunpowder, making it likely that the burning fuse would extinguish at that point. When I looked into the bag containing the bomb for this operation, I saw that the safety-fuse was not in coils, but was bent and kinked repeatedly. I did not say anything, because I was not an expert and the bomb-maker was set to be my teacher.

I duly planted the bomb one day, ignited the fuse, waved to my companion, and then left the building. There were less than ten minutes to go before the bomb's detonation and I walked around nearby waiting for the arrival of the police and army.

After some crucial minutes, nothing had happened. I began to get worried – I was learning that collectivity had its drawbacks. Had the other man phoned the warning? Was the pay-phone which he had been planning to use actually working? Had someone else been using it when he got to it? All of these were possible reasons for the delay, but there had been too much delay already. I began to feel a panic rising in me. If this bomb went off before the building was evacuated, there would most definitely be a lot of innocent casualties. Had the police decided to ignore the warning in order to allow such casualties as would definitely harm the IRA's cause in Derry?

I looked at my watch again. What was happening? There were less than three minutes to go, and even if the alarm were raised right now, it might be difficult to get everyone out of the building in time. This was bad, and might get a lot worse. I was in full panic now, almost to the point of wailing. The warning was supposed to make everything okay! What should I do? There was no phone nearby, and I had no number for the building; time had almost run out and a warning would not help at this point; I felt like crying because I was set to witness a catastrophe that had not been deliberate. I looked at my watch – the bomb was going to explode in less than a minute.

I gazed at the building in a dreamlike state of terror, fear and disbelief, and waited for the explosion. Now! It should happen now! The other night while I worried that the fuse might have burned out, it exploded. This one should go off now!

I could not look. I walked out of the area. I prayed harder than I ever prayed in my life – God, don't let this accident happen, even though we wanted the bomb to explode! Don't let it happen!

This would be the end of my life. I would not be able to live with the guilt of blowing up innocent people. It did not matter that we had given a warning by telephone, which was proof that we had not intended to kill or injure innocent people, nor did the collective nature of the effort dilute my own personal sense of guilt. This would be the end of everything. How would I ever rid myself of the guilt of this slaughter?

I walked and kept on walking, listening for the crunch of the detonation and for the sirens and horns of ambulances and police vehicles, but they never sounded. I slowly came back to myself. Nothing had happened and it was now at least five minutes after the bomb should have exploded. No fuse, even a damp one, could burn so slowly as to take an extra five minutes!

I walked back in the direction of the building, frightened lest any moment the planted bomb might explode and end my rising hopes, but nothing happened! The bomb was definitely not going to explode now.

My recovery was swift, maybe too swift. I chided myself for the panic which had taken over. Praying to God again was surely a bit much Shane! God wasn't some one-armed bandit in the sky who paid out every time you yanked the handle! Get a grip!

In the evening I reported back to the senior officers. They were furious with me, having concluded that the reason there had been no explosion was that I had lacked the nerve to light the fuse of the bomb. I was not, they thought, the operator I had claimed to be.

I was furious in my turn. I explained that I had looked at the safety fuse in the bomb and that it had been kinked in many places. They rejected this as a slur on the bomb-maker and questioned my qualifications to criticize his work. I doggedly held to what was the truth, that I had ignited the fuse. My credibility was being eroded nevertheless by the consensus that the bomb must have been perfect, and that I was the only weak link. The bomb-maker was summoned and rejected any possibility that the safety fuse was to blame for the bomb's failure to explode.

I raised the question of why the police and army had failed to evacuate the building after receiving the telephone warning. The senior officers were puzzled about this, but concluded that they could no longer rely on the Royal Ulster Constabulary alone to take bomb warning calls. The man whose task it had been to telephone the warning call did so and spoke to the desk officer who answered the phone. The desk officer may have simply regarded the warning as a hoax, or he may have desired casualties to harm the IRA. From now on, they said, they would telephone a number of different organizations with bomb warnings, possibly including the local newspaper, to ensure that there were independent witnesses to the fact that warnings were being given. But they still thought that I had not had the courage to ignite the fuse, that my nerve had cracked at the crucial moment. They did not see this alleged weakness on my part as providential, despite the fact that the failure of the bomb to explode had saved lives and injuries.

It was at this point in the dogged argument that I was vindicated, and in such a way that they and the bomb-maker had to apologize to me for the way they had treated me. The wife of one of the senior officers, thinking that we were merely engaged in political discussion, brought in a tray of tea and informed us that the television news had just broadcast a report that a bomb had been found in the government building, with its fuse burned out! Concern was being expressed that no warning had been given.

Three things were now clear: I had ignited the fuse; my criticism of the way the safety-fuse had been kinked was correct; telephoning the police alone could no longer be regarded as a safe method of delivering bomb-warnings.

I left the house with the bomb-maker, feeling on top of my little world, having forgotten entirely how I had panicked about the potential loss of civilian life at the moment when it was clear that the building was not going to be evacuated. The focus had been on me and my nerve, on the make-up of the bomb, and on the method of having bomb-warnings acted upon. There had been no focus on the fact that only a miracle or wild chance had prevented the deaths and injuries of very many Derry people. And so we went on about our business, troubled neither by the catastrophe that had nearly happened nor by the fact that it had been prevented only by a fault in the make-up of the bomb.

After this, I concerned myself primarily with learning my trade. I met the bomb-maker one Saturday morning to learn how to make incendiary devices, and he sent me off to a nearby house to collect a parcel for use in their construction. I called at the house and asked a man for the package. He got very embarrassed and looked worried and asked me if I could call back later for it. I said I couldn't. He then walked some way down the street with me and told me, "The missus found the parcel, opened it and threw it away. I can't replace the contents – there's nothing I can do about it. Tell the explosives' officer I'm sorry. She'll keep guns or explosives for The Cause, but not what was in the parcel."

I went back to my teacher and told him, not knowing what had been in this parcel, but thinking it must be very dangerous indeed, more dangerous even than detonators if the woman wouldn't let it in the house. It must be very high explosive or something similarly lethal.

My teacher was nonplussed and couldn't restrain his frustration, "That was a gross of condoms! How the hell am I going to find a gross of condoms in Derry for crying out loud! Plus I'm going to be blamed for stealing them! Oh fuck! Stupid woman could have kept them for The Cause, dammit!" He was taking this very seriously indeed.

"What's a condom?" I asked.

"Oh fuck! You want to fight for Ireland and you don't know what a

THE VOLUNTEER 57

condom is?! Kathleen Ni Houlihan has marked you for herself!" He began to comb his fingers back through his hair and pace up and down the floor, swearing and trying to figure out where to get more condoms.

"Listen, Shane, here's a tenner. Go round various chemist shops and ask them if they stock condoms, and buy as many as you can."

I said that was fine, and I set off to the Strand Road to Sweeney's Chemist shop almost at the bottom of Clarendon Street. I waited my turn in the confines of the tiny shop I'd used all my life, and asked the lady, "Do you stock condoms?" She reddened and said, "We don't." "Do you know anywhere that does?" "No, I don't," she replied, at which point the pharmacist himself came out to the small counter and asked me, "What do you want them for, Shane?" I said, "I don't really know. A man asked me to buy him a tenner's worth." "Who is this man?" he asked in a concerned manner, and went on, "I think you should tell your parents that a man has asked you to buy condoms with money he gave you. This is a very serious matter."

I was by now too mired by the whole business to want to argue about it any further, so I assured the chemist in front of a queue of customers that I would tell my parents and left.

I tried another chemist nearby, where I got a stiff denial that condoms were stocked, and then a last one, where I changed my tack with a girl server who was about my age, sixteen: "A tenner's worth of condoms, please." "I don't know, but if you'll just wait, I'll go and ask," she smiled. She returned with a man, who addressed me, "What did you ask for?" "A tenner's worth of condoms, please." "Do you know what a condom is?" "No, I'm just running a message for the man next door." "Well, we don't stock them, and I don't think you're going to find any. You should return the money to that man and tell him I said he should go his own messages." I said I would and went off back to my explosives' teacher, still knowing nothing about condoms except that women wouldn't have them in the house, Catholic chemists in Derry definitely wouldn't stock them and the IRA needed them pretty badly... intriguing, really...

My explosives' tutor had managed to find a small number of them, sufficient for the purpose of showing me how to make powerful incendiary devices. He also told me the use for which condoms were originally intended, which caused me an agony of embarrassment when I thought of the questions I had asked in chemist shops where I and my family were well known... A tenner's worth indeed! The Stud of the North... The Flying Stud Column... The Stud Active Service Unit... All of these jokes were applied to me for some time by my friends and I bore them with ill-concealed embarrassment...

Having learned how to make very simple and effective incendiary devices, I and others were sent out to use them, and it wasn't long before I found out that they were very dangerous to the maker and planter, never mind to the general public.

They relied for their fuse-delay on the time which it took sulfuric acid to dissolve two layers of condom, after which the acid ignited the incendiary material with a loud crackling noise and fierce flames. But the acid and the condoms were difficult to regulate and the first accident happened in the city centre to none other than my explosives' teacher, who heard the crackling beginning in a device in his coat pocket and pulled it out to throw it away, but not before it burst into flames and burned his hand. He ran away from the area and sported a bandage for some time. This accident in no way deterred any of the rest of us from making, carrying and planting them in local shops where they caused some spectacular fires. If anything, the accident was a grand joke and served to mark of our bravado that we continued to use the devices.

However, the problems of regulating the timing of their ignition and the worse problem of getting people to store the boxes of condoms generally militated against their regular use, and it was not too long before the development of an electric model which was much safer, though still as potentially dangerous as any home-made device necessarily is.

I also learned how to make nail-bombs, which were simple yet terrifying. A stick of gelignite in the centre of a beer can full of six-inch nails explodes and blasts the nails in every direction. Some time after there had been street rioting one evening, I took my first nail-bomb to the corner of an alley, lit the fuse and threw it at a group of soldiers who had begun to relax. I was running away before it exploded – the troops had hit the deck when it fell fizzing near them. A staggeringly loud boom echoed across the night. The following morning I went to the spot where the nail-bomb had landed and examined the astonishing pattern which the nails made in the tarmac into which they had been blasted. I rarely used nail-bombs because they were generally too heavy for me to throw any distance. I was quite skinny for my sixteen years.

I saw two Army jeeps parked along the cathedral railings one morning and ran off to get a large nail-bomb. It was contrary to IRA orders to use Church property for attacks, but that didn't stop me. I brought the "nailer" along the other side of the railings behind some bushes, lit the fuse and lobbed it over at the jeeps and the soldiers who were standing idly around them. As I ran off through the greenery, the troops must have seen me, but would have been unable to open fire as they scrambled for cover. The nail-bomb exploded in a deafening detonation and I thought to myself, I'm getting the hang of this! I had in mind that I might be shot dead during these attacks, but I was already glorying in their heroic nature and in the martyrdom which I would earn.

We took even crazier risks against the British Army. Small caliber revolvers were available, which were only accurate or lethal at fairly close range, and so I and some others, armed with these, hid in back alleys and waited for the last soldier of a foot patrol to pass by, whereupon we jumped out and blasted off as many rounds at him as we could before escaping up the alley and out of sight, and in particular before the highly trained rifle-man could return fire. It may be difficult nowadays to believe that inexperienced youths could pit small revolvers against rifles in the hands of trained soldiers, but this actually happened. I had never fired a revolver in training, nor had anyone I knew. We hoped to hit.

I had temporary control of a .38 Special revolver and a bag of ammunition and I was insanely heroic in a suicidal sort of way with it, until one report made me wiser. After a riot one evening, and while the British Army was still holding its anti-riot positions along William Street, I took my revolver to an alley near where some soldiers, armed with rifles, were standing at a corner. I waited until I could see that they were definitely not looking in my direction, jumped out and fired all the rounds in the chamber at them, and then ran like hell. I could hear the shouts of the soldiers as they reacted to the attack, and the shouted commands of officers to their men.

Even this insanity was not enough for my patriotic excess, so I reloaded and some time later made my way to another alley near a different William Street corner where more soldiers were on standby. Completely caught up in my own little war, I didn't realize that I was the only person around in this no-man's land where the rioting had earlier occurred, and that I was being watched by Army snipers with night-sights. I didn't remove the revolver from my coat as I hung around waiting for an opportunity to fire. I could see the soldiers and they could see me. After a while I went off the idea and left the area.

I got a shock the following evening to learn from Senior Officers that people living in William Street, beside the soldiers, had been standing at their front doors after I had fired the first shots and clearly heard Army snipers saying to their officers that they had a youth in their sights who was acting suspiciously. They also heard the officers saying that they should open fire if I produced a gun. I meanwhile had been unaware that I was in the night-sights of the Army snipers. I had to think about this close call, and weigh the worth of my life against the importance of the action against the British Army.

The fact is that I really didn't value my life particularly highly at all, that I was prepared in my youthful passion to lose it in any kind of action against the British occupiers. I was more than willing to embrace martyrdom and the place it would win me in the eternal memory of my people, but I had to admit that I should take more care and be aware that the British Army was not playing games.

My first IRA training camp occurred around this time, and I duly informed my parents that I was going off to spend the weekend with friends in Dublin whom I'd met in the Gaeltacht. In reality, I was to go with others to a small village outside Derry and lurk around the main street until cars came to transport us to the farmhouse where we could be given more specialist training in weapons and explosives. I went with my friends from the Waterside section which I had lobbied to leave, and we decided that we should merge with the trees and bushes just outside the village in case we should attract unwelcome notice. It was not difficult for me to merge with nature owing to the fact that, despite every cautionary instruction to dress normally, I had given in to temptation and donned a green combat jacket, combat trousers and army boots, all of which were sizes too big for me!

We waited for hours and no-one came for us, whereupon the Section Leader from the Waterside told us to make our way home, which was a considerable walk, particularly in boots and clothes the wrong size. I don't know what I'd have said to any army or police who might have stopped me and asked questions about my uniform, but luck was with me and I got home determined never to wear that getup again. I was able to change my clothes prior to appearing before the family to say that I had been unable to hitch to Dublin. I was told the following day that the drivers of the cars had driven the length of the street at different times without spotting any of us, and had left under the impression that we hadn't turned up! Our camouflage had worked too well! This story of the excessively cautious Derry unit which had gotten too camouflaged in the countryside caused some laughter for months...

The second training camp pick-up was a success, but the training was a disaster for me. The Training Officer insisted on having a night exercise, and would not hear my explanation that I was night-blind, that is, of perfect eyesight by day, but blind as a bat in darkness. My friends knew my handicap and one promised to lead me, but everything went wrong. I fell over every obstacle in my way, bumped into everything bigger, and fell down an incline into a pool of water before the T.O. would accept that, away from the city street-lights, I could see nothing. I was allowed to return to the farmhouse with my friend as guide, while the rest were dragged across country carrying their loaded rifles.

It all seemed so pointless to me. I was a city boy, and my training should have been city oriented. I had no intention of ever attempting to fight blind in the countryside, especially at night. My friend and I sat and drank tea before the turf fire in the farmhouse for the couple of hours that the rest were abroad.

Some time after they returned, it was announced solemnly that the Chief of Staff of the Irish Republican Army was going to make a personal appearance at our training camp, which must have been one of the first to happen for Derry volunteers. We were stood to attention in a line with me at the very end and waited for the great moment. In came a man of medium height, short hair and sparkling eyes with a determined military air. Two huge bodyguards dwarfed him. He came along the line asking a question of each volunteer until at last he reached the man beside me. My heart beating in my breast, I counted the moments until I would actually meet and be acknowledged by Sean MacStiofain himself, whose whispered name had every patriotic aura and mystique attached to it. I rehearsed my lines, "Yes, Sir, I am a patriot! I want to fight for Ireland! I am prepared to die for Ireland!" These would surely mark me as officer material.

I couldn't believe it when he turned without speaking to me and announced to his guards that he had to leave straight away. I was inclined to be quite cheeky and passionate, and I felt immediately that I could say, "Hey, you! I've probably planted more bombs and fired more bullets than you ever have!" I didn't, and nursed my disappointment quietly. My friends had to comment that everyone had been acknowledged but me. I thought this was my punishment for my unmanly night blindness.

No training camp was ever complete without "stag duty", which meant guard duty outside during the night hours to watch for the arrival of police or army. This effectively meant that any car, cars or jeeps which approached on the very isolated road leading to the farmhouse were to be regarded as hostile and the alarm was to be raised so that weapons and explosives could be moved out fast. This was fine in theory, but problematic in practice since it was difficult to gauge the distance and intended direction of sweeping headlights across country and since no-one could see where the isolated road ended and any other one began, with the result that alarms were raised every twenty minutes and no-one got any sleep. Stories were going to recur of shots being fired by alarmed sentries at hostile intruders behind hedges who turned out, upon hasty investigation, to be curious cows... and, needless to say, the shots missed.

Back in Derry, an outdoor training operation was planned for the centre of Creggan one evening. It was to be a show of strength in public, and a definition by the fledgling Provisional IRA of territory. All of the IRA's available weapons and most of the ammunition were brought to a house in Central Drive and the senior officers and others armed themselves and ran across the street to a large area of grass adjoining a church and school, where they proceeded to slither along on their elbows and knees towards the centre of the field. I recall that there were small American M1 carbine rifles of considerable age, a Thompson sub-machine gun that would have been of more use in a Chicago museum, and perhaps an ageing Garand rifle and possibly an equally old .303. Not being an officer, I was not allowed one of these choice weapons, nor was I permitted to take part in the exciting crawl over the grass. I was ordered to stay at the perimeter.

The fact that there was no cover whatsoever on this field in the centre of residential Creggan, that army jeep patrols might at any moment appear on the roads around it, that a large crowd of astonished onlookers quickly gathered at the shops overlooking the field, and that no-one knew what would happen if a jeep patrol did arrive, quickly communicated to the officers that maybe it would be a good idea to call a halt to the exercise before it got out of hand. The crawling officers had now reached the centre of the grass, and were expected to crawl back again.

An officer on the perimeter told me to make the crowd of onlookers disperse, and I went over to them sure of my ability to do this. I pulled out my revolver, waved it in the air and shouted, "Get off the streets! Get into your homes!" Not only did they not disperse, they crowded around to view my revolver. I waved it around more angrily and shouted again, "This is an IRA operation! I am ordering you to disperse to your homes!" They even laughed! A man leaned over, caught my wrist and said in my ear, "Don't ever hold your weapon away from your body, or someone might take it from you. Keep it close to you, pointing away, then it's safe." He kindly released my wrist, I thanked him and immediately did what he said. The crowd buzzed around my revolver like bees around honey. It was a fiasco...

By this time, the armed officers had reached the house from which they had originally emerged and would be getting the weapons away by car to a safe dump. I was free to go, taking my revolver with me to my own dump.

Fiasco it may have been, but it had also been an historic evening. Here at last were armed IRA men publicly visible in the Catholic ghetto, not afraid to stage a patrol on the streets which the British Army also patrolled. The crowd of onlookers would publicize the news around the entire city within hours, and the story would grow dramatically in the telling, until perhaps a Brigade of armed IRA men had taken over Creggan! For the nascent IRA, it was a necessary first crawl before a more confident stride into an urban guerilla campaign, but there were some losses to be suffered before that confidence would be gained, and they were not long in coming.

One week, I had temporarily hidden a bag of .38 Special ammunition in my bedroom, and, while I was away at an IRA training camp, my sister had been searching for something in my bedroom and found the bag of bullets. She told my parents, and I think my eldest brother dumped the small bag in the nearby River Foyle.

Upon my return home on the Sunday night, and unaware of the find in my bedroom, I was confronted by my father who stated his belief that at my age I must be a member of the Fianna, the youth wing of the IRA, which was not much more than a scouting movement. I agreed with him that this was the case, and that I was only temporarily holding the bag of ammunition for someone else. He said that it was totally wrong for the IRA to exploit someone as young as I was to hide bullets and said that it was unfair to the family to involve them in anything by hiding stuff in the house. If the house was searched, he argued, and if something was found, the whole family would pay the price for one member's involvement in the IRA, and that was not just. I agreed. He made me promise not to bring anything home again, and asked me to keep out of the Fianna. I instantly gave him my solemn word that I would never go back to the Fianna – this was easy, since I was not a Fianna member. I never did bring anything home again, but I did go back to the IRA, about which I had promised nothing. I just had to be very careful about seeming to lead a normal existence outside home and I succeeded in doing so. My cross-country running, choir practice and boys' club activities always furnished excuses for time spent outdoors.

My hero and friend of these months was Eamonn Lafferty, commander of the Creggan unit to which I had been most recently assigned. He was young, handsome, intense and utterly dedicated to freeing Ireland from British occupation. He actually lived very near Clarendon Street, but I always knew him to stay in a particular house in Creggan from which he directed, and participated in, an increasingly aggressive campaign.

When I met him, I insisted that he should not discriminate against me because of my youth, that I had operated more than most people, and that I was determined to be in action. He laughed and took this very well and asked me if I'd do something for him. I said I'd do anything at all. He told me that someone had become frightened about possible surveillance and had dumped a bomb behind a wall of the City and County Infirmary at the top of Clarendon Street where I lived. Could I go and fetch it safely? I assured him that I could and went off immediately.

It was a simple matter to scout the area, climb the wall, find the shoulder-bag bomb in bushes there and carry it back to Creggan. Eamonn was pleased that I had done it quickly and without any fear and promised me that he would not hold my youth against me. I was certain that he was in his twenties, such were his maturity and seriousness and his ability to command.

However, almost as soon as I had earned my way into Eamonn's trust and confidence, I was betrayed. I was informed one evening that a leading Sinn Fein person wished to meet me with a view to converting me to politics, and, more immediately, to having me work in the pirate Radio Saoirse (Freedom), then broadcasting from around the Rathlin Drive area.

I had no option but to go along and meet what turned out to be a suitably serious, tweed-jacketed, slightly balding and priest-like bachelor figure for whom Sinn Fein was everything, and the IRA but a temporary mechanism which might help or obstruct Sinn Fein's political rise. Despite the way in which I have described him, he was a gentleman of some considerable learning and political cunning, with a forward view of events and I immediately liked and respected him.

He told me everything that I didn't want to hear: I was a St. Columb's College boy, he said, with a good education and intelligence, from a good family. Would I not accept, he asked me in a welter of sincerity, that anyone could fire a weapon or plant a bomb, but not everyone could be a political activist capable of being trained to fence with the likes of John Hume and British politicians? Could I not see the tragedy in all the youthful talent going into the IRA instead of into Sinn Fein? Was not the IRA but a temporary tool, while the whole forward vehicle of Irish Freedom was the Sinn Fein political party which was to march into the future? Did not Sinn Fein have a claim on the young blood which was flooding into the IRA, with a view to training it for politics? Could I not see that for all the armed struggle which would happen, nothing would be achieved without a strong political party to translate the Republican ideals into reality in the political sphere? Where would the political negotiators come from when the time for gunfire and bombing was over? Where would the political leadership originate, if everyone ran off to play with guns and bombs? He allowed me to speak.

"No," I said, and continued, "I could not be in a shirt and tie with a political folder in my hand, while my friends were fighting, and maybe dying on the streets. I could not be apart from a military Rising if it happened. I can understand your point of view, but I am an activist, not a politician."

He was annoyed with my answer, but smiled and said, "Well, you're not an activist any more. You're attached to me until further notice." He named the person whose order had detached me temporarily from my unit, and I had no option but to obey. I felt betrayed.

The result was that I had to hang around with this celibate Sinn Feiner, had to meet his arguments and listen to his world view, had to jockey some discs for the pirate radio, read requests, and go off and do some interviews of interest. I recall the most moving interview I did, with an old man in the Brandywell, Barney Gilmour, who had suffered serious injury when a British soldier fired a rubber bullet into his stomach at point-blank range. The old man's voice broke as he told of the incident and of his utter powerlessness against the British Army. I was furious with myself for holding a tape recorder. As if a tape recorder could hurt the British Army!

The result of the interview was that I told my Sinn Fein commissar that I could not stand by while the Brits did these things, that I was reporting back for action and he could do whatever he wanted about it. I said that if young people like me did not stand up to the cutting edge of the British Army, then we were a defeated people, and I was having none of that.

I reported back to Eamonn and poured my heart out and demanded to be allowed to operate. He laughed at me, as usual, and said that I was back if I wanted to be back. I could have cried for joy. I was almost immediately set to carrying shoulder-bag bombs to various economic targets, with a girl for cover. We planted these bombs at different innocuous buildings usually in the late evenings when no-one was around, walked away, and heard the bangs some minutes later. It was nerve-racking at the time, wondering if police or army would discover me carrying the bomb, wondering what would happen if they did. But it was also somewhat stale, since it was becoming commonplace.

I began to notice the changes that were taking place in what had originally been a very small IRA world in Derry. When I had planted my first bomb, the IRA's operators could have been counted on the fingers of two hands. Now there were lots of people coming and going all of whom were available for operations. And planting safety-fuse bombs required little knowledge or expertise in explosives, so more people were getting access to bombing operations. I was in no way central to anything. There seemed to be a very large number of people volunteering for weapons' operations, using rifles. I felt I should stake my claim to operational status by being available virtually all the time for whatever was going on, but there was competition for action.

I was taking my "O" level examinations in June 1971, and had done very little academic work, so I set myself to read as much as possible in Brooke Park library adjoining the perimeter of the ghetto. I distinctly recall one morning (while I studied alone in the reference library with the window open to let in air) being startled by the perfect rattle of a Thompson machine gun some streets away, and I was entranced and put off study for hours. I sat there looking at the dead leaves of the books while one part of me argued, "Out there history is happening! History is being made, and you're sitting in here in your ivory tower studying for exams that will do you no good whatsoever when your number's up! You could have fired that Thompson, Shane! You can probably guess who did fire it! And if there is something on the news this evening to the effect that your friends were shot in a gun battle, what will you feel about your books then? Eh?"

I stayed on, but only just. My attendance record at St. Columb's College at this point must have been pretty bad, though I did often stay for roll call, then left immediately afterwards. I could not live with the thought that something historic might be happening outside while I sat over books inside...

July and August of 1971 were set to be pivotal months of the troubles, but we players did not know that. I distinctly remember one afternoon in July some time after the Army had shot dead a local youth, Seamus Cusack, at close range, claiming that he had been holding something like a weapon. Local people hotly disputed the allegation. I knew that he was not involved in anything. In response to his murder, a number of larger nail-bombs were to be thrown at a huge Saladin armored car on Leckey Road. I had a nail-bomb, but I knew that I would be unable to throw it the requisite distance owing to its weight, and because, on this occasion, I was frightened. The clatter of nail-bombs exploded together in a resounding detonation and pall of smoke on and against the Saladin, which was damaged. Yet almost simultaneously there sounded the cracks of a British Army SLR (self-loading rifle). Within minutes we learned that a soldier in an adjacent street had fired his rifle into a crowd of people when he heard the nearby explosions. A youth, Desmond Beattie, died shortly afterwards from bullet wounds.

I melted away from the scene and hid the nail-bomb and returned to look at the pool of blood where the youth had fallen. I was shocked to see just how much blood was spilled on the paving stones, never having realized how much blood a body contained, and horrified by its turning darker and darker as it dried. Someone had already placed flowers near the spot and within days there was a little cross there. I was glad that I had not thrown my nail-bomb, but confused about the relation of the incidents.

The British Army released a statement that the youth had been holding a nail-bomb, but the claim was patently untrue and did a lot to enrage the local people, and me. It was clear to me that the British Army was sending a macho message to the ghetto by way of these shootings, and I felt a youthfully passionate burden to be one of the defenders of my people sending replies in kind.

These two British Army murders of local youths fixed the parameters of the IRA campaign in Derry for some time to come. While Belfast had bitter sectarian troubles, with Protestant and Catholic mob violence paralleling the IRA campaign there, the Derry IRA, already practicing the bombing of economic targets, was set to try to confront the British Army as much as possible and make it pay for these murders. Sectarian religious murders were almost unknown in Derry then as now, unlike Belfast and some Border areas. The Derry Brigade of the IRA thought that it was duty-bound to take on the British Army in ambushes and gun battles, but guns were in short supply.

Also in July, a child was crushed to death against a wall by a British Army lorry in Westland Street and a fierce and bitter reaction occurred. I went to the scene and found armored cars and soldiers confronting the frustrated local people who felt that here was yet another case of the foreign army, once accepted as protectors, now responsible for the death of a third youth in virtually the same street within a matter of days. This did not need to be expressed in words – it manifested in youths climbing onto armored cars and trying to tear them open, trying to trap the Saracens with stone blockades, throwing stones and petrol bombs at other army vehicles and setting fire to the death lorry.

These were the events in Derry which preceded the introduction of internment without trial on August 9th 1971, the other big event that changed everything. It had been rumored for some time and the IRA leaders were telling us that it was imminent and they were not living at home, but staying in safe houses. On the day, one of my friends from my previous Waterside unit called at my home early in the morning and said, "Have you heard the news? Internment has begun!"

We were very excited and rushed off to a contact house in Creggan where all the IRA faces I expected to see were present and correct. Fierce rioting was occurring everywhere, at the perimeter of the Bogside and Creggan, at Bligh's Lane army camp, at Rosemount police and army barracks, everywhere...

I found Eamonn and asked him what was happening. He was determined and busy and said, "Everything's happening! The gloves are off!" A tough, no-nonsense operator said that he was taking a powerful revolver to a corner near where there was usually a lone, armed soldier on sentry duty close to an army post. He said he was going to jump out and try to shoot the soldier before the soldier could shoot him with his rifle. I asked if I could go along and he said I could.

On the way to the corner, I asked, no, I begged to be allowed to fire the revolver. My companion liked me, and knew that I was desperate to operate, so he agreed, but only on condition that I fired all the bullets in the chamber when I jumped out. I assured him I would, even though I knew that there was no chance that I could squeeze the heavy trigger six times. I expected to get three shots off before having to run like hell. A trained soldier with a rifle was no dodo...

A ferocious riot was going on nearby, but we skirted this and made our way to the corner of a street of small, terraced houses. I glanced around the corner and, sure enough, there was a lone soldier with a rifle standing guard near an observation post. I gripped the revolver and steeled myself, but my heartbeat was racing. You want to get your own back for your people's suffering, now's your chance, I said to myself. The fact that he was holding a rifle and that his reactions were trained blunted my courage some.

I walked around the corner before I wouldn't be able to and, as ever, everything slipped into a dreamlike slow motion. The problem was that my eyes immediately met the soldier's eyes. He showed no shock or fear, just calm. Meeting his eyes, I forgot all about the revolver and aiming it. I fired once, and again, but heard nothing whatsoever in the dreamlike unreality. He began to slide down the wall he was leaning against, but his facial expression had not changed, nor had his eyes left mine. He still held his rifle pointing at the sky. He can't be much more than my age, I thought. As this dreamlike scene seemed set to continue, a hand yanked me back into reality.

I was running up the street as fast as I could alongside my companion. I couldn't get the big revolver into my pocket as I ran, so it was visible. From the corner of my eye I noticed two girls watching us from a doorway. I thought I recognized one, and I knew she recognized me – it pleased me considerably to be seen in such a heroic pose. Then we were around another corner and I got the gun into my coat. My companion complained, "I thought you said you could fire all the rounds! You only fired two! Did you hit him?"

"I don't know! I think so! He slid down the wall!" I didn't say that I'd only seen his eyes.

We got back to base to find everyone out and about with every kind of weapon that was available. Reports came over the news that a total of five soldiers were shot that day, one seriously, and one who had been shot twice in the leg. My companion said that the latter was mine. If he was, I was glad that he was not seriously wounded, because I had looked into his eyes and seen a human being behind the visor, rifle and uniform.

It is difficult to describe the effect of internment on the entire Catholic population in Derry. The headline across the front page of the local newspaper, "The Derry Journal", read "LEADING DERRY CATHOLICS WITHDRAW FROM PUBLIC POSTS – INTERNMENT, REIGN OF REPRESSION DENOUNCED".

Thirty-two prominent Catholics holding public appointments, including Churchmen, Justices of the Peace, members of Derry Development Commission and of the Police Liaison Committee, announced in a statement across the front page of the local "Derry Journal" newspaper:

"We totally abhor and condemn the introduction of internment without trial as a gross violation of natural justice. We abhor and condemn all the more the glaring partiality with which it has been applied and the inhuman treatment of many of the victims and the violation of their homes. We furthermore denounce unreservedly the reign of repression now in effect in this city, culminating in the humiliating treatment meted out to our elected representatives and other responsible citizens yesterday, while taking part in a perfectly peaceful protest. For all these reasons, we, the undersigned, feel bound to make the only protest available to us, namely to withdraw forthwith from undermentioned positions we hold in public life."

The paper was filled with accounts of the local community confronting British soldiers, CS gas canisters being fired into homes, shooting incidents, protests, and of some sixty Derrymen being kidnapped by the Army in the raids for internment. Feelings can also be gauged from the uncharacteristic statement released by the veteran peaceful Nationalist Party leader, Eddie McAteer, on the arrests of the two Members of Parliament:

"Shame on the British Army of Occupation for this day's work. Leader-snatching will not blunt our resistance. Open war was declared on ordinary people with not a gunman or a stone-thrower in sight, and all to prop up another tottering Orange Chief. I call on the Irish people to stand fast against the dying kick of British Imperialism. Show them your feelings in any way you can think up. Let the British Army know it cannot beat Derry to its knees."

It was in the wake of the internment trauma and the military attempt to crack down on the ghettos that Eamonn Lafferty, myself and many others were steeling ourselves to go out against the British Army.

We had a verbal agreement with the much larger and much better armed Official IRA in Derry regarding the night-time patrolling of the barricades. I should explain that there were sizeable barricades at the perimeter streets of the Catholic ghetto areas, particularly in the wake of internment, which the British Army usually would not cross until the middle of the night when they would raid homes to arrest and question people. At night, the Official and Provisional IRAs mounted mobile patrols aimed at offering resistance to British Army incursions into the ghetto. The Officials had real weapons, like AK47 assault rifles, and some "heavy" stuff, including at least one Browning .500 machinegun. It was suspected that they had a bazooka too, and a personal friend of mine in the Official IRA had spoken with me about trading items for ammunition which they lacked. Eamonn Lafferty and I had stopped and talked with them at the Broadway barricade in Creggan and looked enviously over their weaponry.

My family was away on holiday in Donegal. I had expressed teenage boredom at the idea of spending weeks in Donegal countryside and said I'd prefer to stay at home ostensibly to find summer work and pocket money in Derry. My father had agreed with my work ethic and allowed me to stay at home. I did find part-time work in a restaurant and so I was making sufficient money with excellent tips to prove that I was not messing around. In reality, I often spent nights at the house where Eamonn stayed, going on patrol in a car with him until the wee small hours, and then at dawn sometimes driving to a bakery in the Bogside for fresh hot "baps" (bread rolls) which we'd eat with mugs of hot, sweet tea for breakfast, before going to sleep. This is what I was doing with Eamonn during the week after the introduction of internment.

A brand new .303 rifle with telescopic sight had come into Derry and Eamonn practiced with it and generally made it his own. He used to carry this when on night patrol. I was with him for a few trips around the barricades and we had spoken to the Official IRA again at Broadway who told us that the British Army was definitely going to come into the ghetto in force to remove as many barricades as possible. They said they would look after the Broadway end of Creggan.

Eamonn told me that he too had learned that a large Army force was expected some time later that night and that there might be some serious action. I was particularly sleepy that evening and he stopped at the house where he always stayed and forced me to get some sleep in a chair in the front room, saying that he would collect me later. I fell asleep in the chair, expecting to be wakened for my share in the action. I was wakened not by Eamonn, but by my explosives' teacher who said, "Shane – they got

Eamonn. Eamonn has been shot dead in a fierce gun battle with the Brits at Kildrum Gardens."

Nauseous and disoriented from lack of sleep, the news seemed unreal, and I barely took it in and left the house immediately. I walked home, which was dangerous and silly, because Army units with mechanical machinery were taking down barricades and were being covered by jittery soldiers who had just been involved in two dozen different shooting incidents. I went home anyway via side streets and climbed wearily into my own bed and slept, weary in body and in spirit. I had no doubt that Eamonn had not wanted me along, because, whatever he said to my face, he did regard me as just a kid. I would not have been prepared or able for the ferocity of the gun battle that night, not least owing to my night blindness.

I woke to the news that indeed Lieutenant Eamonn Lafferty was dead, killed in action defending Creggan, the first IRA volunteer to be killed in a gun battle in Derry. He was nineteen years of age. Attached to this news was another item that the British Army had also inexplicably shot dead a deaf mute man, Eamonn McDevitt, in Strabane. Feelings were running as high as they possibly could against the Army we had such a short time before welcomed as defenders of the Catholic community.

Barely did I catch my breath on these killings when I got news within hours that another of my friends had been shot dead in a mysterious incident in the Waterside. He was Jim O'Hagan, sixteen years old, who had become my friend while we were in the Waterside Section together, and whom I'd met on the street only a few days before.

Reports began to circulate that the interned men had been tortured by soldiers and policemen after their detention and during the most brutal interrogations. One story, later confirmed during hearings before the European Commission of Human Rights at Strasbourg, was that at least two well known Derrymen kidnapped for internment had wooden broom-handles forced up their rectums along with other tortures in the name of law and order. The outrage was growing in the Catholic community which was just realizing the implications of the internment raids, primarily that no-one was safe from the British Army. The British Army could break into any home, rush upstairs and drag husbands from their marital beds before screaming wives and children. Men could be taken off for torture that included "white noise" disorientation, blindfolding, beatings and threats of being dropped out of helicopters from a great height, followed by indefinite detention without trial – a fitting monument to Britain's claim of a peacekeeping role in Northern Ireland. This was a license to rape a community.

All of this swelled the ranks of the mourners at the huge IRA funeral for Eamonn Lafferty, a funeral that became for me, and for some of my comrades, the occasion for extreme bitterness against both the remote leadership of the IRA and the local leadership of the Catholic Church.

I and others of Eamonn's friends were told that we should not attend his funeral, that we could not form the masked and uniformed color party for it and that outsiders were coming in to run the funeral... This made me very bitter.

We learned that Eamonn's coffin would be lying in the Cathedral overnight before the funeral and we wished to place the Irish tricolor flag over his coffin and pay our respects in our own way. I went off and got a tricolor flag from a Nationalist Party family and an older, taller well-known Brandywell volunteer and I proceeded to the parochial house beside St. Eugene's Cathedral, where I had been baptized and confirmed and where I had also been a choir-boy for some years, in order to tell the priests what we wanted to do.

We rang the doorbell and out came the Bishop's hatchet man, a priest who didn't have any time for the IRA and for whom the IRA was about to have as little time. Though much younger than my companion, I explained what we wanted to do, and the priest immediately refused to allow us into the cathedral or to have any militaristic or paramilitary ceremony whatsoever in the cathedral.

My big friend then spelled out to him that other coffins had had British Union Flags draped over them both inside and outside the Cathedral. This rattled him some. The argument went on for some time, and I lost my temper and told him there would be extremely bad feeling about this slight to a dead IRA hero, a local boy, whose family lived barely a hundred meters from the Cathedral and who had earned the right to some payment of respects from his friends. He gave in, and said we could go to the coffin, pay our respects, leave the tricolor on the coffin overnight, but must remove it before anyone arrived in the morning. We agreed.

Big — and I went over to the Cathedral building and entered by a side door, went quickly to the coffin, placed the tricolor over it, paid our respects and were just leaving with the hatchet priest when he told us (he had been prowling around outside) that the Army must have spotted us and were arriving at the gates around the grounds of the Cathedral. He quickly got us out a side entrance and we got away.

Early in the morning, before the funeral, I went to the Cathedral once more, removed the tricolor and returned it to the family who had loaned it. I went back to view the outsiders who were running the funeral. When the coffin came out of the Cathedral, it turned out that they had no tricolor with them for the coffin, and I had to run off about a quarter of a mile to get the original one from the family again, and then run back with it and hand it over to these buffoons. I did so and then couldn't watch as they marched, out of step, along the roads towards the cemetery and through the thousands of Derry people who thronged the streets. "Can't even march in step!" I thought in disgust. I left.

For some years I thought that after Eamonn's death I fell away from the IRA in bitterness and because the huge influx of volunteers into the ranks of the IRA had sidelined me somewhat. I now see from the local newspaper reports of bombings that I was planting bombs for about another ten or twelve weeks. For instance, in just forty-eight hours a week after Eamonn's funeral, six bombs exploded in the city centre damaging many premises.

One evening around this time, I intended to plant a bomb in a government building, next door to a brightly-lit shop. I was going to light the fuse on my quite unwieldy ten-pound bomb and then throw the bomb through the ground-floor window and run like hell. I found someone who agreed to drive me to the area, but before I could set off, I was told to take another operator along who would plant a bomb at the large shop next door. We were in the car and on our way to the targets when I noticed that my companion's bomb was improperly fused, such that the matches would not ignite the gunpowder core of the safety fuse. I pointed this out to him, and gave him my device, thinking that I could ignite his fuse by some method or other.

We arrived near the targets, and the car departed after disgorging us. My companion walked to the showroom, lit the fuse on what had been my device, saw it fizz, placed it in the shop doorway and then ran off across the street into the darkness and away. I meanwhile struggled to light his useless fuse as I stood on the pavement beside the government building in the bright lights of the showroom. There were window-shoppers in the distance on the other side of the street, but no-one else was near, although there was a long line of parked cars.

I suddenly noticed from the side of my eye that one of the parked cars about a hundred meters away was screeching out onto the road and beginning to race towards me. I realized immediately that this was an unmarked police car put there for the very purpose of watching for would-be bombers of this government building and the shops beside it. In the instant that I saw the car scream out, I darted across the main road and into a side street where there were many parked vehicles close together. I hid down behind one of these right at the junction, clutching the useless bomb. The unmarked police car screeched around the corner, passed my hiding place, but stopped just along the street in a squeal of brakes, when the occupants realized they had lost me.

In that moment, I thought I would have to give myself up – the police were armed and I was not. If I tried to run away, they would surely shoot me in the back. I visualized in a microsecond my court appearance a few days later, the response in my family and in Derry generally, and my subsequent imprisonment. But then I visualized the police shooting me dead – why should they take me prisoner, since I had been caught red-handed in a bombing operation? There was now no way that I was going to give myself up, and I decided to run around the corner back onto the main road, and sprint along to alleyways that I knew well. I knew if I could just get around the corner, the police would never catch me. I darted to the corner, hearing a "Halt!" command behind me, but I was around and away before anything else happened. As I sped along the road, I remembered the other bomb whose fuse had been lit and which must be due to explode any moment. I ran into another side street, heading for an alley which would save me, when there was the boom of the exploding bomb, and the sound of glass and masonry falling and crashing. That would keep the police busy. I was free! I had gotten away, seconds after I had had the thought of giving myself up!

I ran on towards the Bogside, sure that if I was determined enough, there was nothing I might not do. I made up my mind never to give myself up, to take the slightest chance that offered, to believe that the police and army would probably shoot me even if I did intend to surrender. That night marked a dramatic change in my attitude – never again would I look to the police or Army for terms.

It is not easy to admit to operations that went horribly wrong for whatever reason, but I have to relate one that did in the first few days of November. I had volunteered to fire a rocket at a British Army observation post high on the historic walls of the city. The operation meant stepping around a corner into the clear view of the Army observation post and aiming and firing the rocket before any sentry could open fire in return.

Late one Sunday night, I was driven to St. Columb's Wells and strode to the corner with the small launcher, steeled my nerves and stepped out and into my usual slow motion view of things. I pointed the launcher at the large post and fired, seeing the rocket-trail instantly traverse the distance and yet rise to miss the top of the post by what must have been a matter of inches. The sweep of the trail went beyond the post and I lost sight of it. I could not believe that it had risen so dramatically and was slow in realizing that I had to get back around the corner, but as I moved I heard a loud boom across the sky. I ran back to the car and jumped in to be driven away at speed, only to hear the harsh cracks of rifle fire somewhere nearby, but not near enough to be fire directed at me. My driver said, "That was a loud explosion! You hit it!" I replied that they always sounded louder at night against the silence. I didn't tell him that it was a mystery to me what I'd hit, but I did comment to him, "I wonder who fired at what." I went soon after to report to the Brigade O.C.

I have to explain that many Derry women from the Bogside and Brandywell were fervent addicts of bingo evenings, and a great deal of gossip – call it intelligence information – was swapped and gathered. In fact, very little that happened in Derry went unmentioned at these bingo evenings. It happened that the O.C.'s wife had just returned from bingo with a report on the mysterious explosion, and he was waiting for my arrival.

When I called to his home, his wife let me in, and her face was signaling that he was in a vile temper and that I was in deep trouble. I went into the kitchen to see him with one hand behind his head ruffling his hair, the other fiddling with the open neck of his shirt – a bad sign. He never gave me a chance to speak, but shouted, "What the fuck have you done? A woman and two children have been shot!"

"Shot? I fired a rocket – " I began, but he cut me off as my stomach began to sink and sicken.

"You fired the rocket! The Brits have shot a woman and two children!"

I began to get angry with this O.C. who had never actually operated, as far as I knew, and who was continually agonizing about a campaign over which he had only nominal control.

"Listen a minute! I fired the rocket. It soared over the observation post and exploded somewhere else, and I heard some shots after that. That's as far as I'm responsible. Don't try to make me responsible for a British Army shooting."

"Well, your rocket exploded on top of another Army post at Bishop's Gate and a soldier fired on a car driving away from the checkpoint, hitting a woman and her two children."

"Go complain to the British Army!" I fired back at him.

"You're nothing but trouble, Shane, you always create trouble! I can't take much more of this!"

It was an open secret that this O.C. couldn't cope with his position and he was destined to give it up very shortly after this incident. I left him and went home, feeling really sick at the thought of the woman and children being shot. I felt particularly guilty because the little girl who had been shot was being described as critically ill and I couldn't face the possibility that she might die. I had moved my bedroom up to one of the attics of our house, and I still recall the agonizing I did that night over the shooting, and my return to the ultimate court of appeal, prayers for the life of the little girl and the recovery of the woman and her boy. I prayed for hours on my knees before my bed because I did not want an innocent child to die for my act against the British Army. The following day brought news that the child was still critically ill, but slightly improved. The boy and his mother had been released from hospital after treatment for slight injuries. The little girl recovered.

A huge row had blown up about the Army shooting, not least because the Army put out different stories just after the event, the first one claiming that a bomb had been thrown from the car. The controversy had become more heated partly because the victims of the shooting were Protestants, members of a community normally giving support to the British Army and usually unwilling to believe that the Army would shoot first without asking any questions, and also because witnesses claimed that the shots were fired up to a minute after the explosion. The fact that the occupants of the car were a woman and two children completely undermined any Army attempt to claim that they had been any way involved in illegal activity. If two or three men had been in the car, the story would undoubtedly have been very different.

For all the political controversy and the mess into which the Army had leaped via its trigger-happiness, I was in some shock over the consequences of my act and rocked to my foundations over the near death of the child. I did fall away from the IRA after this incident in early November, and also because there were so many new, more mature IRA volunteers in the wake of internment and the various Army killings. My previous importance, limited though that might have been, had disappeared. For all that I have recounted, I was still only sixteen years old and very much looked it.

It is a myth that an IRA volunteer cannot leave the IRA. Any IRA volunteer may cease to volunteer his or her services, the only remaining contract being that he or she should keep trade secrets, which is hardly surprising. Not only may IRA volunteers leave the IRA for whatever reasons, whether nervous, religious, family, or romantic, but they may be thrown out for a host of reasons, including drinking, indiscipline, bad time-keeping and general unreliability, etc. As the ranks filled, so they were constantly culled to remove the blaggards, the big-mouths and the downright dangerous. I just drifted away in November and didn't report back to compete for operations. Nobody noticed. They saw me around anyway from time to time as I walked to and from St. Columb's College every day.

CHAPTER 4

Bloody Sunday

So Christmas came and went and a New Year dawned, 1972, and my seventeenth birthday came hard on its heels on the 25th of January. Four days before my birthday, the headline across the front page of the local "Derry Journal" on was: "GET OUT" CALL TO BRITISH ARMY – "OVERWHELMING CATHOLIC MAJORITY REGARDS YOU AS ENEMY" – DERRY NATIONALISTS' OPEN LETTER TO AREA COMMANDER.

The open letter to the army Commander read in part:

"For over a year the British army has conducted a campaign of intimidation, oppression and outright terrorism against the Catholic people of this city. Eighty per cent of the population of the west bank of the Foyle, that is, the overwhelming Catholic majority, now regard your army as their enemy and as an army of occupation.

All the protests from many quarters about army savagery in Derry, whether they were from the 32 prominent Catholics who withdrew from public life and spent four hours detailing to an unresponsive General Tuzo exactly why, or the complaints of revered priests, or the frustrated warnings of political leaders, or the heartfelt pleas of suffering men, women and children, have gone unheeded, and your army has pursued a course of action that has created a situation in Derry filled with the possibilities of major disaster.

You, as commander, have the ultimate responsibility for the excesses of your troops. The ordinary British soldier must accept an individual responsibility when he brutalizes a helpless man, but responsibility becomes greater as rank becomes more elevated. Know this – whatever your intelligence sycophants may tell you to the contrary, the antipathy to the British army in Derry is not confined to people your propaganda machinery refers to as "hooligans". It is deeply rooted within the entire Catholic community. The truth of the terrorism of your army may not yet have got through to the British people. But the people of Ireland know what your men have done. The people of the world in general more and more hold Britain in contempt for what is being done in this partitioned part of Ireland. You may raid, you may arrest, you may intern, you may shoot the Catholic people of Derry. But you can never remove the stain of dishonor the British army has earned on the streets of Derry."

The possibilities of major disaster in Derry and the truth of British Army terrorism were to be fully realized nine days later.

The Civil Rights Movement had spearheaded and organized the massive street demonstrations against internment, and one was planned for Derry five days after my birthday, on January 30th. Seventy-two hours before the march, a police car driving on Creggan Hill, which was part of the march route, was ambushed by at least three IRA men with machine guns. Two R.U.C. men were killed and a third injured. One of the dead, a sergeant, was a Catholic. Two days before the march, the "Derry Journal" reported on its front page: "Army build-up for Derry Civil Rights March Reported". The report included the lines:

"Amid reports of a big military build-up in the Derry area and that the British army is determined to prevent a breach of the parade ban by even stronger methods than the demonstrators at Magilligan experienced, the Civil Rights Association last night issued an appeal to all who take part in the demonstration to observe discipline and allow any breaches of the peace to be on the part of the British army."

I attended the march with Eamonn, a son of the Nationalist Party leader, to whom, in spite of his odious pacifist conviction, I was prepared to be a good friend. The march was huge, and wound its laborious way from the Bishop's Field, Creggan, via William Street – where the British Army had set up barricades to prevent Derry Civil Rights marchers reaching their own city centre – one day these soldiers were taking down barricades, the next they were putting them up – and then to Free Derry corner in the Bogside where the crowd was to be addressed by Westminster M.P.s and Lord Fenner Brockway, the Labor peer.

Eamonn and I were dawdling along well to the rear of the march, when our group reached the barbed-wire barricades where British soldiers of the paratroop regiment, already wearing gas masks and holding rifles, were confronting us. It was pretty normal to reach the barricade and then wend on to the speakers. Younger elements were inclined to stay at the barricades shouting at the soldiers, demanding to know why Derry people should not be free to march into their own city centre, etc., but this was all par for the course.

As Eamonn and I reached the wire, I noticed a big, hefty guy on my right-hand side wearing a handkerchief over his face who pulled out what was obviously a CS gas grenade (a long rubber pouch, with grenade-like ignition device attached to it). He lobbed it over the wire barricade and into the soldiers where it gave out clouds of white gas. Since the paras were all wearing gas masks, I found it incredible, but my instant reaction – and that of everyone else – was to get the hell out of there before being choked by the gas. We all pushed back and began to go up William Street to Rossville Street. It was not possible to run owing to the crush of the crowd.

As we got to the Rossville Street junction and entrance to the ghetto, we heard the screaming whines of army vehicles and loud bangs which we thought were rubber bullets. Everyone began to run fearing that the Army was sending snatch-squads to arrest people. I had been a cross-country runner at St. Columb's College, and I took off across Rossville Street with Eamonn somewhere behind. The bangs had turned into sharp cracks, and I knew immediately that high velocity rifle fire was being directed all around us, not the blunt bangs of rubber bullets. Everyone else seemed to realize it as well.

Thousands of Civil Rights marchers, men, women and children, not long after their Sunday lunch, fled in waves before Army paratroopers who were firing indiscriminately. Everyone felt that something was terribly wrong with this. There could be no reason to fire into a peaceful crowd. Innocent civilians were being killed around us and the rest of us had to find cover before we too were shot dead. Many hundreds of people lay on the ground screaming at everyone else to do the same. Others ran on towards little courtyards between nearby houses and, as I ran to the arched entrance of one of these, bullets hit the brickwork, but I wasn't stopping. There I realized that Eamonn wasn't with me, and after hanging around for a few minutes, I ran on to Eamonn's house, thinking that we should meet there. People were shouting comments to each other, and I gathered that many persons who had been around me at the Rossville Street junction, but who couldn't run as swiftly as I had, had been seized by the paratroopers.

I arrived at Eamonn's home and found his brother who was a priest. He had already heard reports of the murders of peaceful Civil Rights' protestors, and feared that Eamonn might be among them. He wanted to go and check the bodies which still lay where they had been shot, and I agreed to accompany him.

We drove down to the Bogside a short distance away. We went right to the "front line" beside the high-rise flats in Rossville Street where bullets had caught up with fleeing civilians and found a most horrible sight. A middle-aged man was lying on the ground in an impossibly huge pool of blood. The back of his head had been shot off, and bone and brain matter lay around. People stood staring numbly at this appalling sight, until the large Northern Ireland Civil Rights Association banner was laid over the body and blood. The resultant stained banner would serve as a graphic reminder of the day's events.

Rumor now had it that maybe as many as a dozen men were dead, with many others wounded. My companion began to panic. He decided to drive across the river to Altnagelvin Hospital in the Waterside to check the bodies in the morgue. I said I'd go with him, but I didn't believe we'd get anywhere near it because of the checkpoints which were by now in operation all over the city.

In actual fact, my companion's priestly garb, his I.D. and conversation with soldiers at the checkpoints got us over to the hospital in record time. As we walked along the shiny hospital floor towards the morgue, I saw top Army and Police officers standing outside it laughing and joking. I said to my companion that I couldn't go into the morgue, but that I'd wait outside for him. For all my IRA activity to date, I hadn't been confronted with death in the flesh, and couldn't face the multiplied version here. He went in alone. The Army and police officers took no notice of me, possibly thinking that I was just a kid.

After a while I saw the first of the relatives arriving to identify the bodies of their husbands and sons. Small older women, supported by sons and daughters, were walked along in floods of tears, unable to believe that their loved ones had been shot dead in the course of a peaceful Civil Rights march. As they reached the morgue doors, they saw the smiling, laughing, joking officers of the British Army and Royal Ulster Constabulary.

I blinked back the tears and felt that there was a reason why I was witnessing this. It was clear to me that I was a fool for having drifted away from the IRA. If I could be shot dead for having taken part in a peaceful Civil Rights march, I might as well be shot for having fought the Army murderers to the best of my ability. I felt now more than ever that it was incumbent upon me and the likes of me, the young men of the people, to take on the role of defenders since the forces of so-called law and order were murdering us. I knew that I would report back to the IRA to compete for operations within days. I now definitely viewed the British forces as terrorists in my country, murdering my people, and violence directed against them as a moral imperative.

My priest companion got caught up in ministering to the relatives of the dead and I had a long wait beside the morgue doors in my festering bitterness. When he did come out of the morgue, he had a notebook filled with the names and addresses of the other relatives of the dead and of some of the wounded, and he asked me to accompany him while he comforted them at their homes. I reluctantly agreed. We set off in sullen silence across the city to the Bogside and Creggan, and called at various homes. The tears and moans of the shocked relatives were too much for me, and I waited outside while the priest went in. It was later confirmed that Eamonn had been one of a group of people arrested by paratroopers after the shootings, and that he was alive.

So, thirteen Catholic people were dead for their crime of taking part in a Civil Rights march, and many more had been shot and wounded. What would it matter if Irish government ministers and others attended the huge funerals? What would it matter if the world's media attended as well? What good would they do the next time the British Army terrorists decided to shoot Catholics?

It would be difficult to exaggerate the anti-British impact of Bloody Sunday upon Derry and upon Ireland. In Derry, as the local paper reported, factories, shops, stores, banks and offices all closed down in protest, and the streets were deserted. Teachers went on strike, and schools closed. Seven local priests who were present during the murders, including the future Bishop of Derry, Edward Daly, published an open letter in "The Derry Journal":

"We accuse the Colonel of the Parachute Regiment of willful murder. We accuse the commander of Land forces of being an accessory before the fact. We accuse the soldiers of shooting indiscriminately into a fleeing crowd, of gloating over casualties, of preventing medical and spiritual aid reaching some of the dying. It is untrue that shots were fired at the troops in Rossville Street before they attacked. It is untrue that any of the dead or wounded we attended were armed.

We make this statement in view of the distorted and indeed conflicting reports put out by army officers. We deplore the action of the army and Government in employing a unit such as the paratroopers who were in Derry yesterday. These men are trained criminals. They differ from terrorists only in the veneer of respectability that a uniform gives them."

Most Catholic homes in the ghetto flew black flags as a protest and sign of mourning. In areas housing both Catholics and Protestants, flying black flags required more commitment, but my father instantly agreed to my suggestion that our house in Clarendon Street should fly one.

This indelibly marked our house as nationalist, and in Protestant minds, as Republican also. Bloody Sunday undoubtedly helped the alienation of the two communities, since one had the opportunity to view the killings as justified, while the other had occasion to feel aggrieved about that. Meanwhile, in the adjoining Irish Republic, a massive crowd protested outside the British Embassy in Dublin and burned it to the ground before the eyes of the Irish police. Ever idealistic about the possibilities, I saw this as a sign that the Revolution could be near at hand.

The funerals of the civilians murdered on Bloody Sunday were attended by Government ministers and Opposition leaders from the Republic of Ireland. They regarded their attendance (many of them were on their first trip to Derry) as a mark of temporary solidarity with the Catholic Nationalist people of Derry. They were given seats in St. Mary's Church in Creggan for the funeral Mass, while Derry people stood outside in the rain and cold. I got angry about that, left the area and retreated into my bitter little world.

The funerals were an anti-climax. I felt that the enormity of the injustice had been too quickly buried. The politicians of the Republic of Ireland could go on about their remote, private business while we once more had to look to the IRA to defend us in British-occupied Northern Ireland.

I reported back to the IRA on the day of the funerals, and was disappointed to find that, as I had expected, it had yet again grown enormously and that it was going to be very difficult to get a chance to operate. I met some older and quite experienced explosives' officers who had been trained in booby traps and anti-handling devices which they attached to bombs. In whispered stories, I heard that they had killed and injured soldiers of the Felix squad, the bomb disposal unit. They seemed so much older than I was, or else I seemed so much younger than they were, and I was offered very little participation in operations. I found it humiliating to know nothing in advance about the very many bomb attacks. I did pick up the very simple method of using clocks and electronic circuitry to detonate bombs, which did away with safety fuse and which allowed refinements such as booby traps to be incorporated. I learned the theory, and was only once allowed to set the timer for a very large lorry bomb which was sent into the city centre and devastated it. I was even more humiliated when the IRA ambushed British Army patrols around the grounds of St. Columb's while I was sitting in class studying for "A" levels in Irish, French and English. I felt very much a civilian and this rankled with me. Our teachers, mainly diocesan priests, expected us to continue with class work while the cracks of high velocity rifles and the explosions of booby traps or landmines split the air outside. For me, it was a superhuman task.

Lord Justice Widgery was appointed to inquire into the events of Bloody Sunday from a safe base in the mainly Protestant small town of

Coleraine. Local people declared this British inquiry into British murders the "Widgery Whitewash" and were intent on boycotting it.

Two of friends of my age, Colm Keenan and Eugene McGillan, were shot dead in March by the British Army some time after a late night gun battle had occurred in the Bogside. They had no part in the gun battle, but had taken cover in a house until the danger had passed, which was not an unusual thing to do, and had drunk tea with the family. As the house owner let them out and as they stepped onto the footpath, concealed Army snipers, still in place since the earlier gun battle, shot them both dead without any challenge or justification. Colm was nineteen. Eugene was eighteen.

When I heard this story, I went with a friend to talk to the house owner, and he told me how he dragged one of the two into his kitchen and found him shot through the head. He had bled copiously onto the floor, moaning, and died shortly afterwards. The graphic telling shook me and angered me against the Army. The fact that the two were IRA volunteers and got IRA funerals seemed to retrospectively justify the killings in the Army's mind, but it remained true that they were not involved in the gun battle and were shot by virtue of the fact that they walked onto the street when the Army had put the area under unofficial but deadly curfew.

The Chief of Staff of the IRA, Sean MacStiofain, attended the funerals and gave interviews to the press about an IRA peace plan. It initially amounted to an offer to suspend military operations if the British Government withdrew British troops to barracks and abolished the Protestant Stormont parliament.

As I struggled to justify the continuation of my studies, a bomb hidden in a car exploded in an alley off Clarendon Street just as a British Army patrol was passing. The bomb injured soldiers, damaged windows and the fronts of many houses and could have killed civilians. I was in the front room of my home studying, and was injured by debris and glass. This was the final straw for my attempt to bear up under my humiliation and alienation from the too-popular IRA.

At the same time, the Official IRA kidnapped and shot dead a nineteen-year-old Catholic lad from Creggan, William Best, who was home on leave from the Royal Irish Rangers, a regiment which did not serve in Northern Ireland. The Provisional IRA was said to have given him permission to come home to visit his family. The reaction in the Bogside and Creggan to the shooting of Ranger Best was fierce. Hundreds of angry mothers gathered and marched on the Official IRA headquarters to protest and scuffles and arguments broke out with leaders. Shortly after this amazing public repudiation, the Official IRA called a ceasefire.

I was not aware of the details of the other public ceasefire which did in fact take place between the Provisional IRA and the British Government from June 26th. It included direct talks between the leadership of the IRA and senior British Government minister, William Whitelaw, in London, to which IRA leaders sported their personal firearms (as one of them told me later). Whitelaw had earlier met with hooded men of the Ulster Defense Association, the biggest Protestant paramilitary organization.

I felt that it was definitely time to have a break from the crucible that Derry and Northern Ireland had become, especially since my own role had diminished to nothing and since the IRA seemed to be getting close to a deal with the British Government. Like many another student facing a summer of unemployment in Derry, I decided to seek summer work (and play) in London, staying with my brother in West Hampstead who worked as a town planner for a borough council. I set off to London and was amazed by its size and by the cosmopolitan nature of its huge population. I was surprised to find that Derry and Northern Ireland, which I had imagined to be the focus of international attention and media coverage, were of no interest whatsoever to anyone. I quickly found a job and English friends and began to enjoy the myriad evening and weekend amusements that were available. I experienced innocent fun, something that I had missed out on, and was so busy with work and new friends that I heard virtually no news about Northern Ireland after the report of the ceasefire.

In fact the ceasefire was doomed to fail and rather quickly, and when I telephoned a friend in Derry in August, I learned that the Catholic ghetto areas, which had since Bloody Sunday been barricaded and termed "no-go" areas – areas which the police and British Army could not enter – had been invaded by the biggest British Army force so far seen in Northern Ireland using fifty-ton Centurion tanks adapted as barricade-busters. Fifteen hundred troops and three hundred army vehicles had broken into the Bogside and Creggan, and the IRA had decided not to fight against overwhelming odds, but to retaliate later. The British Army was now in effective control of the ghettos, but more in the manner of an occupation. During "Operation Motorman", as the invasion was called, troops had shot dead two teenage boys in Creggan and wounded some others, and a girl had suffered a rubber-bullet blast at point-blank range.

I now found that my hopes for an end to the conflict, that the ceasefire might work, were so much wishful thinking. I tried to enjoy to the full the time I had remaining in London and then I returned to Derry for school at the beginning of September. I remember trying to find out about different universities in the London area, a sign that I hoped to get away from the conflict after my "A" level examinations.

The city I returned to was very different from the one I had left. A sense of occupation was definitely in the air. Soldiers on the streets were cocky and aggressive, undoubtedly because they felt that in Operation Motorman they had achieved a victory over the people the IRA claimed to defend and champion, and therefore over the IRA.

I found out just how cocky the troops were a mere four weeks later. I had walked a girl home before midnight and was returning to Clarendon Street. My letter, which was published in the "Derry Journal" on October 3, 1972, tells the story:

DERRY YOUTH'S EXPERIENCE AT HANDS OF BRITISH TROOPS
Sir,

As I walked towards the sand-bag emplacement along Asylum Wall, opposite where the Society Restaurant used to be on the Strand Road, at 12.30am, Sunday, I was told by one of eight or nine British soldiers to raise my hands as he wanted to search me.

I raised my hands automatically and this British soldier bent down, as I thought, to begin by frisking my legs. He lunged forward from a bent position and knocked me full length on to the roadway in rugby style. I hit the road bearing his weight and hurt my left wrist.

An officer, wielding a small leather baton, came forward and stood over me flicking his baton against his thigh. The soldier got up and said: "Did you try to kick me just then, eh?" I didn't answer and managed to get up at the second attempt, nursing my wrist.

The soldier ordered me to put my hands on my head and I had great difficulty in doing this as I had sprained my wrist. The officer asked me where I lived while the soldier searched me, still inquiring if I'd tried to kick him. I told the officer I lived in Clarendon St. and his attitude changed somewhat. He told me to "get" and hit me with the baton as I made to go. There were no witnesses present except for the rest of the soldiers, who took great enjoyment from the incident.

I can only warn young people of my own age to be wary of walking alone around midnight, or indeed any time. I will never again be surprised at stories of British army brutality. I made no complaint to the so-called authorities because of the helplessness of my position.

> Shane O'Doherty
> (17 years)
> 39 Clarendon Street,
> Derry.

I actually wrote a much tougher letter than this. I claimed that when I said I lived in Clarendon Street, a "nice" area, the Officer immediately told me I could go, and I recommended to other young people from the Bogside and Creggan to say that they too were from Clarendon Street – but the paternalistic "Derry Journal" edited out my youthful sarcasm. In fact, the Editor rang Eddie McAteer, President of the Nationalist Party, about the letter because they both knew my father. Eddie spoke to me that evening and asked if my father knew that I'd penned the letter to the newspaper. I lied and said that he certainly knew. Eddie said that was fine and went back to talk to the Editor on the phone. The letter duly appeared a few days later.

At St. Columb's College, I was summoned from class by a prefect who told me that the college president, the Reverend Monsignor James Coulter, wished to see me immediately in his office. I did not like Monsignor Coulter one little bit, finding him an extremely snobbish, class-conscious priest who had often expressed, not in so many words, displeasure at the fact that St. Columb's had taken in riff-raff from the ghettos.

I went to his office and he threw a copy of the "Derry Journal" across his desk and said, "You have brought this college into disrepute!" I had already lost my temper in anticipation of this very remark, and because I felt that I represented the oppressed, ghetto people before this remote Catholic monsignor.

I replied that the college wasn't even mentioned in the letter and asked him to comment on Army violence done to college students. He replied merely that the letter would bring me lots of trouble. We did not agree and called it a day, but I knew that Coulter didn't want me in the College any more. I'm sure he'd gathered where my loyalties lay. I went home at lunchtime to find that my father was annoyed, but only about my failure to tell him that the letter would be printed. His fellow teachers had come to express their support for me, and he was embarrassed that he didn't know what they were referring to until they showed him the paper.

As Monsignor Coulter had predicted, the letter did bring trouble my way, primarily because it published my address. As I left my house after lunch, I decided to walk to St. Columb's via the city centre, whose shops and shoppers made it a more interesting journey. I didn't at first notice that two Army jeeps were trailing me from Clarendon St. – the traffic hold-ups and general activity hid the fact for a while. I was distinctive enough in my St. Columb's College uniform, carrying an armful of books, to be visible from a distance. Eventually, in Shipquay Street in the city centre, it dawned on me that the jeeps had slowed to my walking pace and, as I looked full at them, they stopped. An officer jumped out, flanked by riflemen, pushed me against a shop front and stuck his baton under my chin.

"Shane O'Doherty, you think you can publish a letter of evil allegations against the Army and have no comeback? Search him!" My books were taken, checked and dropped on the pavement, and I was searched minutely, in front of passers-by, many of whom knew me. The officer, meanwhile, continued his threatening tirade.

"You are clearly a Republican sympathizer, and perhaps more than that. We will watch you constantly, follow you constantly and we will deal with you the first wrong move you make. We have you in our sights. You will be sorry for publishing your propagandist lies."

It is important to remember that, following the break-up of the no-go areas, the IRA had all but left Derry for the safety of Donegal. The Army believed that it had achieved a lasting supremacy and was reacting quickly against any sparks which might ignite a new flare-up. I was told to go, collected my books and walked, shaking, the rest of the way to school. I took this kind of intimidation in public very seriously, because the heavy implication was that I could be shot dead for my ideology. This was not a game, and a warning was to be taken as final. I was experienced enough to know that there was no court of appeal here, that it was the Army versus me, and that I alone would have to make any decision that might affect my safety or survival, such as leaving Derry. Asking older people, even relatives, for advice, was pointless, since they had no experience of this conflict.

I met Una, the girl I was seeing then, and, after an evening together, I walked her home via Duncreggan Road past a base for the Ulster Defense Regiment. The street lights had been switched off to obstruct any snipers who might use nightfall to ambush cars going to or from the base, and as a result the road was in total darkness. As Una and I walked down the pavement, two jeeps stopped across the road and we were approached by soldiers with torches. It was the Army officer who had stopped me on the street and he shone his torch in my face.

"We'll see you on your way home, you bastard!" He and his bodyguards went back to the jeeps and drove off. It was true that I had to come home by the Northland Road, since the other route, Strand Road, was where I had been beaten up.

Una, who lived on the Culmore Road well away from areas of trouble and who had no experience whatsoever of any street conflict, was distraught at the threat made by the army in her presence, in the total darkness of Duncreggan Road and in the absence of any witnesses. I tried to calm her by denying the seriousness of the confrontation, and walked her home. However, I now felt the full implications of the Army officer's threat and I telephoned my friend, Eamonn, to tell him about it. He borrowed his father's car and collected me.

The Army knew where I lived and that fact made me accessible at any time, coming or going – there were checkpoints at the end of my street. They knew the parameters of my existence – my school and my girlfriend. At the moment, they were reacting to my letter to the local paper, but I was getting warnings which were deadly serious, and failure to act on them could be fatal. I felt, as I had done on Bloody Sunday, that I could be shot for nothing, or I could be shot for as much as I could possibly inflict on the British Army, and I chose the latter. While I felt I had no option but to leave home and Derry, I was loath to do so. I decided to ask advice of the IRA commander who was then a few miles across the Northern Ireland border in Donegal. He was not a Derryman, but someone drafted in from Belfast to attempt to organize the new IRA in response to Operation Motorman. He knew nothing whatsoever about me, had more problems on his plate than I could imagine, and treated my halting reference to the Army's verbal harassment as a minor issue, probably exaggerated by the teenage youth in front of him. His advice, however, was that I should decide for myself, because I knew best my situation.

I decided in principle to leave Derry and go to Dublin where I could stay with the two friends who had asked me to join the Provisional IRA two years before. I didn't want to tell my family about the threats from the Army, not least because if they protested about them, they too would become the objects of Army harassment. I had made the decision to go, but I thought that if I waited a little longer, some unforeseen solution might occur to me.

I managed to get to and from school the following day without any visible attention from the Army, but as I reached the porch of my home, an adult neighbor, who was a Protestant and, as far as I could determine, a part-time volunteer member of the Ulster Defense Regiment, came up to me and asked me about my letter to the paper. He wanted to know if it was genuine, if I really had been beaten up, and why I had published the letter instead of going to the Royal Ulster Constabulary to make an official complaint.

I answered him as best I could, but he paid scant attention. "There have been a lot of bombing and other incidents around here recently," he said, "almost as if someone from here were supplying the information for them or even carrying them out himself. You'd better watch your step, Shane." With that, he walked away.

I took this as a final warning. I had very little time to act. I spent some time in idle conversation with my parents and kid brother, went to my room and took what few items I wanted and left the house without saying anything to anyone. I knew when I left home for Dublin that my family would quickly surmise that I had gone for reasons related to the IRA. I had to go, and it was better to go cleanly, without long drawn-out scenarios. Many families in Derry had had to deal with news that their son had been shot dead. It was not so bad, I told myself, that my family would awaken to the fact that I had left home. I would have a friend tell them that I was in Dublin where it was safe, and where there was no paramilitary activity or danger from the Army. I saw everything with the terrible youthful intensity, and thought nothing more about my family's reaction.

When I got to Dublin, I felt an overwhelming sense of relief at escaping the British Army's threat against my life. I moved in with my two friends and their camaraderie made the transition easy. We found some casual work on building sites which paid the rent and left some spending money. It was not so bad. Some weeks later, as we talked of politics and violence, we began to wonder if it was right for us to be in Dublin, far from the trouble affecting our people, when we might be back in Derry, this time as full-time IRA volunteers engaging in daily clandestine armed struggle, moving from safe-house to safe-house. I did not feel that I was cut out to skulk around Dublin. We decided to go back to Donegal to ask the IRA commander about it.

The interview with the IRA commander was short and to the point – he did not want our services. We drove South again. It was late at night when we approached Dublin, I was asleep in the back seat of the car, and I did not notice that the driver was also falling asleep. The car slowly left the road and hit a number of concrete fencing posts along the edge of a field, and then turned over a couple of times. I awoke in the darkness to find that my neck was hurt and that I could barely move it. A number of cars travelling behind ours had witnessed the accident, and one of them took me to hospital in Dublin. I had a neck-brace fitted and was put to bed on my back with strict orders not to move, and told that I would be there for some weeks. I did not realize that my eyes were terribly blackened and gave the false impression that I had been severely beaten.

The Irish police arrived next day to enquire about the accident and the stolen car. I didn't even know that the car had been stolen by the guy who drove us to Donegal! I told them that I was merely a hitchhiker. They left in no doubt that I had been beaten up as a result of some internal IRA business.

Two weeks later when I was quite improved, a nurse told me that the police were coming the following morning to take me away for further questioning. I upped and left that night, and went to stay with a girl I'd met years before at the Irish summer-school in Donegal. Later I stayed with relatives in Dublin while my neck healed and even got a job in ITT's Yellow Pages where one of my duties was to accompany a girl to the bank on the ground-floor of the building to collect the wages.

Then I heard that a prominent Republican from Derry was being held by police in Dublin, and I decided to visit him pretending to be his brother. I got in to see him and told him that I wanted to be back in action in Derry, but this time as a full-time IRA volunteer. He said they'd be glad to have me, and directed me to see a certain person in Derry. I said goodbye, feeling better than I had for some time, and was promptly grabbed by two Special Branch officers who viciously bundled me into a nearby room for the hard man/soft man treatment. I told them angrily that I hadn't experienced such treatment even at the hands of the British Army and that they should be ashamed of themselves. They let me go.

I went to say goodbye to the girl I knew in Dublin, and promptly set off to Derry, this time to a safe house in the Bogside, with the exciting prospect of full-time service in the IRA. The only drawback was that, as I'd so recently seen, the British Army had achieved a measure of supremacy in the ghettos by virtually occupying them during and after Operation Motorman, and my life-expectancy, whether in strictly physical terms or in the rather more loose terms of active service longevity, was not very great.

I arrived in Derry in January of 1973, and waited to be contacted. Eventually, someone came to say that there could be some long-range, single-shot sniper attacks to get things going. I got together a very good false I.D. and began to walk around the Bogside and Brandywell areas which were to be the horizons of my world and my battleground. I was introduced to various families whose doors were always open to the IRA, and these safe bolt-holes were the oxygen of the nascent campaign. With this network of hidey-holes mapped in my mind I began to look around for opportunities to attack the British Army, and I had the strong feeling that the Army Officer who had taken advantage of his power to harass me must now allow me to respond in kind. I was no longer tied to a home address, with predictable movements, and vulnerable to threats from any booby in uniform. I was now going to amass as many attacks as I possibly could against the Army before the Army got an opportunity to kill me. This was my sole raison d'être when I turned eighteen. I asked a relative to tell my family that she had seen me and that I was safe and fine, but not to give any other information about me. This was cold-hearted, but it made my life easier. I could no more afford to hang on the feelings of my family than a youth who had joined the Army or the priesthood – I had given myself up to the IRA and that was that.

As far as I could determine, there seemed to be only five or six operational people left in the Bogside and Brandywell, and I preferred this smaller, tighter IRA. It was a time when one had to rely on the local people for everything, particularly for silence, since almost everyone who was interested would know within a very short time who the operators were. Two of these were girls, and they came to tell me that they would have an

ArmaLite rifle and ammunition ready for me if I wanted to try a single-shot sniper attack against an Army patrol. I had looked over the Bogside pretty well and noticed a house that commanded a long view across which Army foot-patrols were sure to pass. We decided to take over the house during an afternoon, and try a shot whenever it became possible.

On the day, I and one other operator, both disguised, knocked at the door of the house and told the occupants that we, as members of the IRA, were taking over their house for a few hours. The people were veterans of trouble, and did not seem terribly upset about it. The girls arrived with the ArmaLite rifle and ammunition. The ArmaLite folded down to about half of its extended size, and was portable under a coat, or even under a long skirt. The drill was to fire the shot, pick up the ejected shell (minding that it would be very hot from the firing), get both to the waiting girls and then move out of the area fast before the Army could get checkpoints and searches underway.

I took the rifle upstairs to the slightly-open window overlooking the view, where I loaded it and got into position. I had no experience of firing the weapon and I was going to use the fixed sights over quite a distance. Before I had time to think, a patrol appeared and I had aimed and fired, shaking from nerves. The sound of the shot cracked across the Bogside, and I grabbed the ejected shell, forgetting that it was too hot to touch. It burned my hand, but I got it and the rifle to the girls who were waiting in the hall. They left, and I went to the kitchen to let the people know that they could go about their business, and I thanked them in the name of the IRA. I left and got out of the area and into a safe house immediately.

The shot missed, but the incident helped to put the IRA back into the ghetto and into the news. Movement became difficult for a time as the Army stepped up patrols and house-raids, but I managed to stay out of their way.

A week or so later, another shot was to be tried in the Brandywell, and I was elected to take it, having somewhat exaggerated my ability. This shot was to be relatively close range, at the last man of a long Army foot-patrol. Once more we took over a house and I readied myself at the window upstairs. The window looked down to a gap between two houses and onto a pavement which the Army patrolled at irregular intervals. I pointed the ArmaLite through the open window at the gap and waited for the patrol.

Eventually, a soldier crossed the gap, and I counted until the last man was to appear, and aimed. I was shaking yet again, but more violently, because this was a hitting range even for someone with no training. He appeared in my sights and I saw his flak jacket and rifle. I did not hesitate. I fired at the centre of his bulk, as we had been taught to do in our first training camps. He definitely went down! I nearly dropped the rifle, forgot to watch where the ejected shell landed, and had to search for it, delaying our escape from the house and the area.

An army helicopter was in the air over the ghetto virtually all the time, and could respond immediately to a radio call from the patrol. It would swoop low over the area and report on the movements of males and of girls who might be ferrying weapons. News travelled fast in the ghetto – when I got to the safe house by a circuitous route, the family was already talking about the sniper attack. An army ambulance had been heard – a sure sign that a soldier had been hit. My arrival shortly after the ambush was a sure sign that I'd had some part in it, but the family said nothing. The media later reported that a soldier had been shot by a sniper, but that his injuries were dramatically reduced owing to the fact that the bullet had hit his rifle first. I was delighted that I had hit a soldier, but not too unhappy at the fact that he had survived, and by such an extraordinary circumstance. I wanted to fight these soldiers of a foreign army, but, in my heart of hearts, I would not wish the individual to die, because in the moment that he was hit, he ceased to be a uniformed soldier, and became a human dreading death and wanting to hold on to life. At the same time, I remembered with bitterness so many Irish who had had their lives taken away by this army...

I got word after this that I would not be required to fire any more shots. Someone had twigged to my exaggeration of my prowess. More people were coming forward, anyway, to get involved or were returning from refuge in Donegal. Once more, as ever before, the IRA was beginning to swell at the grassroots.

There was by now an increasing number of IRA volunteers, but the Army was capturing them on a regular basis. One evening we intended to have a meeting in a house in the tiny Brandywell area, which was hotly patrolled by the Army, but which gave almost total support then to the IRA. I was picked up late by car and I thanked my lucky stars for the fact, because when we neared the rendezvous, the Army was raiding it. We managed to drive out of the area. One of my very good friends was arrested at the house and I later read his account of his interrogation. He was taken for a car ride through the most strongly Protestant area of the Waterside, and threatened that he would be handed over to Protestant paramilitaries, while detectives squeezed his testicles in an effort to get information from him.

Another of my good friends, who sometimes shared not only my safe house, but the double-bed as well, promised to waken me early one morning to take me to a house in the Bogside where there was a possibility of getting involved in some action. In the morning, he decided not to waken me, but to let me have the luxury of a sleep in.

He went off to the house, from which he was plucked by SAS men who used a furniture removal van as cover to drive into the Bogside. My friend later died in Long Kesh internment camp of an untreated asthma attack. Such arrests occurred with regularity and were a major spur to me to clock up as many operations as possible before my turn came. I became so involved in my local war that I couldn't have told anyone what was happening politically in Northern Ireland or in the world generally.

I got roped into a large-scale robbery operation, where a substantial pay-roll was to be "liberated". We were to meet in a house in the Bogside which had often been raided, but were not expected to stay long there. I stood behind the venetian blinds at the large front-room window watching an Army foot-patrol wend its way along the street outside. I had just turned away after seeing the last soldier go by when one of the girls began to check a large pistol, pulled back the slide, but let it go, whereupon it fired with a huge BOP! The bullet whizzed past my ear and out the window. The girl screamed, dropped the pistol and ran for the back door. The Army patrol on the pavement outside was the problem. I grabbed a broom and smashed the window where the bullet had exited, to destroy the tell-tale spider's web of the bullet-hole in the glass in case the patrol found the source of the gunshot. I then grabbed the empty shell which the pistol had ejected, and gave it and the gun to another girl and told her to get them out of the area. Then I too got out. I'd already forgotten that I had almost been shot through the head.

I now got the time and opportunity to specialize in explosives' work. I made up dozens of bombs for others and suffered many a "gelly" headache, that is, an incredibly throbbing, excruciating migraine from the heavy, marzipan-like fumes of the gelignite. There were days when I walked from a bomb-factory to my safe house in the Bogside or Creggan almost blinded by the ferocity of the gelly headache, and looking as pale as a corpse. These nitroglycerine headaches lasted for hours.

On one occasion, someone I knew complained to me about the huge bombs which were being left in the city centre adjacent to the shop in which he worked. He was aggrieved that some of the IRA persons who had driven the bombs into the busy shopping street had left the trucks and then entered his shop to give the impression that they were there on legitimate business and to negate any suspicion about their leaving the lorry. They had told him about the bombs and had then left the shop to return to the ghetto. He, meanwhile, had to remain in the shop until the alarm was raised by the IRA telephone warnings, and he said his nerves could no longer take the pressure of knowing that people were coming and going unawares around such huge bombs. I made some critical remark about his lack of courage, at which he got very angry and left, and did not talk to me for a long time. I had no appreciation of his more mature, experienced worries. The irony is that all these years later, when I have ceased to support the tactic of violence, he does support the IRA, because his son is deeply involved in it, and he has made critical remarks about me!

At this time, I heard that my father had been taken ill and had been hospitalized. I went home very carefully one evening, and saw my mother and sister. I later went to the hospital to visit my father, who was obviously close to death. He recognized me and repeated his hope that I might be safe. He died on May 17th at the age of sixty-five, a month before his retirement as Principal of the Brow of the Hill school. I was able to attend his funeral without difficulty.

Some time earlier, in tandem with the older, more experienced explosives' operators, I had put together a crude letter bomb, which was sent to policemen and others. None of the first rudimentary devices worked, but they did get a whole lot of publicity. Within days, an electronically detonated letter bomb had been developed along extremely simple lines.

A week after my father's funeral, I was showing someone how to make a letter bomb in a kitchen in Creggan. I had just put it into an envelope and sealed it, when I patted it. As I looked at it, a rainbow seemed to rise from it and speed past my head, quickly followed by a blue light, then an almighty BANG! I was blown over the chair, and rose unable to see from one eye and with terrific pain in my right hand. I was bleeding from different perforations around the face and eyes. What I could see was all red, owing to blood in the uninjured eye. The person with me was unharmed, but shocked, more so on seeing my injuries, which looked worse than they really were. He ran outside and literally hijacked a van, brought me out and took me to an address I gave him, where I knew I could get medical treatment.

One eye was seriously damaged; I could see nothing from it; one finger was very badly blast-damaged, and I was being advised that I would have to lose it; the hand surrounding it was quite badly injured also. I had lots of little pieces of metal in my face, chest and eyelids. I refused to accept that I was going to lose the finger. I was given an injection of pethidine and shortly thereafter felt no pain. At this point, I just had to come to terms with possibly never seeing out of my right eye again. As ever, I counted myself lucky to be alive, and thought of friends and others who were dead, and who would treasure life even with my injuries, and I acclimatized easily, perhaps too easily, to being injured.

A friendly doctor brought an eye specialist to see me and the verdict was that I had damaged my sight to a degree that would only become apparent when the eye healed – there was no real treatment available for it. The finger was still in doubt, but the surrounding injuries, having been cleaned and dressed, had healed quickly, though leaving obvious scars and discoloration. Two weeks later, the bandages were taken off my eye and I could see very little. My finger was still giving cause for concern, and I decided to go to Dublin and seek some treatment there. I got over the Northern Ireland border without difficulty and made it to Dublin, where I sought treatment. My eye improved steadily and the hand wounds healed, but I still bear the obvious scars.

It was while I was recuperating, and slowly getting my vision back, that I met one of the top IRA people in Ireland who talked to me about letter bombs, and about the fact that the Price sisters and others had been arrested shortly after planting bombs in London in March. Would I, he asked, be prepared to go to London to send a wave of letter bombs to prominent targets, since, as he'd heard, I knew London pretty well?

Without a moment's hesitation, I agreed to go, honored at being chosen for active service in England, delighted at the prospect of getting centre stage to myself, enthralled at being given the opportunity to attack the most prominent people in Britain. Attacks on soldiers seemed to me by now to be fairly unproductive, since the British Government regarded soldiers as expendable by virtue of their working class origins. If the sons of the high and mighty were being lost in Ireland, I often thought, the British would have withdrawn from Ireland long before. Why should not those in government and in high military and political circles face the consequences of the British military occupation of Ireland? Why take it all out on an eighteen-year-old kid from an impoverished background by taking his life away? It seemed more just to take the war to London.

CHAPTER 5

London Bombings

As soon as I was fit, I prepared for the easiest and yet most important operation of my IRA career. The logistics were very simple: I got five hundred pounds sterling in cash, about two pounds of gelignite and black gelatin, with two dozen electric detonators. I put the explosives at the bottom of my deep rucksack, but slid the detonators into its tubular frame in case the baggage was x-rayed. I got a good false I.D., the background to which I learned in some detail, so that it would certainly hold if checked, and then flew to Heathrow, where I collected my bag without any difficulty. My big rucksack had gotten through both Dublin and Heathrow airports unscathed, with the explosives and detonators intact.

I had told absolutely no-one in Ireland that I was going, neither family nor friends. I just disappeared from Dublin and was gone. There was no doubt that the British Army, police and intelligence services would be very quickly aware that I was operational in London – just as many people in the IRA would quickly work it out as well. There are certain traits and behavioral characteristics surrounding operations which identify the operators. With the usual amount of loose talk in the IRA in Derry, and with a panic-stricken response by British security personnel, I would shortly be somewhere around the top of the wanted list, with too many agencies to be considered after my scalp. It was a thought which heightened my desire to accomplish as much as possible before the inevitable capture or killing.

I went to a flat rental agency, and took a small apartment with its own front door in West London, and moved in immediately. It was important for security reasons to have my own front door, so that any visitors I might have would remain unseen by others. I was a wealthier student from Ireland attending the University of London, if anyone was asking. I was in place as simple as that. I went shopping to procure the common electronic components I needed for the letter bombs, and set about making as many as possible, before my nerves were tried too far. The accidental blast hadn't deterred me from making bombs, but it had shortened the time I wanted to spend working with them. I now needed regular breaks to steady my determination.

I had been given a verbal brief as to my targets: government ministers, military top brass, major institutions and so on. This was primarily a publicity-grabbing operation, with as much disruption as possible. A few waves of letter bombs, and some smaller time-bombs, would create a wealth of international publicity and bring to the attention of the world that Britain had many skeletons in its Irish cupboard which had not had a just burial.

I had in mind my own agenda, with, at the top of my target list, the British government minister who was responsible for security and the military at the time of Bloody Sunday, the former Conservative Home Secretary, Reginald Maudling. He was the only individual who was a specific target. (Just after the Bloody Sunday murders, Bernadette Devlin, M.P., had attacked Maudling in Parliament and scratched his face.) Most of the rest were targets by virtue of the particular office they held.

I wanted a letter bomb to get close to Maudling, and I didn't care if it detonated. I just wanted him to receive it, as my personal protest against the Bloody Sunday murders I had had to witness. I wanted him to know that Bloody Sunday was not buried out of sight in the past. I decided not to send one to his parliamentary office, nor to his town address or club, but to his country house, where he might be caught off guard. I also decided to send one to 10 Downing Street, the British Prime Minister's official residence, not really believing that it would ever get inside. I thought the British Army's London Area Command O.C., who had, incidentally, been in charge of security at a recent Royal wedding, should also be addressed a letter bomb, and I looked up his name. He turned out to be one Brigadier Michael O'Cock, which I thought was an extraordinarily Irish name.

The Director of Economic Intelligence at the Bank of England, a similarly prominent individual at the Stock Exchange, a Military Intelligence officer at a British Embassy, and a Senior Chaplain to the British Army, who had been reported as saying that the Army had done nothing wrong on Bloody Sunday (a press misrepresentation which had not been clarified in Ireland, where the comments attributed to him had angered a lot of people), were among those who were targeted.

Having experienced the effects of a letter bomb explosion myself, I didn't believe that they would ever kill, and none did. I did accept a very remote possibility, however, that they might kill. I expected that after the first wave of letter bombs, most people would be on their guard and that succeeding waves would be intercepted, but that the publicity value would still hold.

I went to the public library and checked "Who's Who" and various Yearbooks, including that published by the Daily Mail, for information on the office-holders and for their town and country addresses. I found "Who's Who" so useful that I went to a bookshop and bought my own copy.

I telephoned my address to a number in Ireland, because I had been told to expect some very limited help from people who didn't want direct contact with me, but who would deliver items of use to my flat. I came home from a shopping trip one evening to find that a package had been thrust through the letter-box. It contained an incredible assortment of unused official and government envelopes, with various stamps and markings, which would make it all the easier to get the letter bombs past security checks, and to get otherwise suspicious recipients to relax their guard. Someone working for the government obviously had sympathy for the IRA cause.

I got ready to post the first wave of devices, realizing that something was not quite right with them. I was unable to find a type of wire that I needed, and had to make do with something inferior. They might not detonate at all, but the mere receipt of them would have the same publicity value anyway. I posted them from various locations in central London. Some required stamps, and there was no problem taking them to post offices to have them weighed. I thought the risk of detection at this stage was fairly remote and I was not nervous. Within a matter of days of my arrival in London, the attacks were under way. From the IRA's point of view, this operation cost them virtually nothing in material or economic terms, and only one volunteer was involved.

I went back to the apartment feeling relieved that I had managed to carry through the first part of the operation, that nothing could now stop it, neither my arrest nor my being taken out by undercover or intelligence people. I went to a small Pakistani restaurant for a cheap meal, and the young, talkative Pakistani waiter suggested that I try some wine. He brought a half-bottle of Sauternes, which I had never before tasted. I agreed and drank it with my meal as a celebration. I went to bed, and tried to quell my nervous anticipation of the news that would certainly break the following morning.

During my active service in London, my private life was monk-like. I hardly ever drank alcohol, and when I did I was abstemious. I had no girlfriend, and didn't go out in the evenings to anything other than a cinema. I lived for the armed struggle and for the IRA.

I had the radio tuned to the LBC station, which focused on news broadcasts and phone-in programs. When the story broke, it took over the radio stations, the front pages of the evening newspapers, and the television news programs. Letter bombs in London! If the IRA had detonated five bombs each of a thousand pounds in Northern Ireland that day, they might have earned a paragraph or two on page five of the national papers, but the sending of two-ounce letter bombs in London to prominent persons and institutions, was regarded as heinous, as unbelievable, as terrible, and as subject matter for a thousand comments on the air and in print!

The following morning the national dailies were screaming the news across the front pages. When Northern Ireland was critically ill from pneumonia, no-one got too worried, but when London sneezed, the whole world was required to look on... I could not believe the publicity generated by the sending of two-ounce letter bombs. I sat in my apartment surrounded by the daily and evening papers, listening to the dramatic radio broadcasts. I marveled at the fact that all the hundreds of bombs I had set off had not together amassed one percent of the publicity given to these tiny devices. I was so sickened by this that I had to go out. I went to Hampstead Heath for a couple of hours where I watched the radio-controlled model boats and yachts on the pond. I thought of Eamonn Lafferty, shot dead in a gun battle by the British Army when I should have been at his side, and wondered what his sacrifice might have achieved if he had been shot in action in central London! The world, at least, would have heard about it, whereas his death in Derry had probably gotten a two-line mention in the press.

Letter bombs had a short life-span, since media warnings put people on their guard against them. I decided to put together a second wave before this happened, becoming increasingly nervous as I faced devices identical to that which had injured me just a few weeks before. With all the explosive and electronic materials laid out on a table, someone rang my doorbell. I took it for granted that the caller was an IRA courier. When I opened the door, I found a young, cheery police constable standing there. My heart fell into my boots, and I was barely able to breathe.

"Hi!", he said, "I'm just wondering if someone by this name is resident here." He held up a summons in an incomprehensible name that seemed like Swahili.

I said, "No, I'm a new tenant, just moved in."

"Sorry to bother you then. Goodnight!"

With that, he went away and I staggered back inside and waited while my thundering heartbeat subsided. I thanked my lucky stars that I hadn't been armed, because I might have panicked and used a gun.

I did not have an inexhaustible supply of explosives, and so I decided to plant very small devices around central London more for the disruption and publicity value than anything else. Bearing in mind the unexpectedly extravagant media response to the letter bombs, small time-bombs, virtually the size of a cigarette packet, and detonated by wristwatch timers, were certain to gain the same publicity. I made up a number of these mini-bombs, and planted them against the petrol-tanks of cars in Mayfair and in other central locations. Sure enough, the first radio reports, which set the tone for all the following reportage, claimed that car-bombs had exploded in Mayfair... On one occasion, I planted a couple of cigarette-packet devices in cinemas in Leicester Square to disrupt the tourist night-life of the West End, and these got the same hysterical treatment in the news. I planted a few devices in Chelsea at addresses I had been given of persons who worked for the British intelligence services and or military or political bodies.

Another evening, I found a package against my front door (which was reached via a small overgrown garden) and took it in. It contained about ten pounds of gelatin in small packets, which gave me the capacity to plant slightly larger bombs. A girl came over to join me temporarily for cover purposes. We decided to plant a bomb in a basement boutique in Oxford Street, and I first of all "cased the joint" so that there would be no mistakes. I checked that there were pay-phones nearby so that I might be able to telephone a warning to the police. The area might then be cleared before the explosion.

On the day, she and I walked the length of a crowded Oxford Street. I was carrying the bomb in a shopping bag, and had it made in such a way that I could insert my hand, set the timer to give an hour-long delay and then join two wires which were the final connection, making the bomb live. We crossed the busy street and stopped at a traffic island. I bent down, inserted my hand, set the timer and joined the wires. The bomb was now set. I was no more nervous than usual.

However, as we reached the crowded pavement, I suddenly felt an urgent need to defuse the bomb, and did so right there. I told the startled girl that we should go to a side-street, where I would be able to take a look inside the bag. I subsequently discovered that I had set the timer to give a few minutes instead of the hour, a mistake that was caused by the clock being upside-down in the bag. I could not understand what had warned me of that danger, which I had totally failed to see when I initially made the bomb live. If I had not felt the urge to defuse the bomb that instant, we would have been blown up by it a minute or two later. I once more fused the device, and we planted it without difficult in the basement boutique. I hurried to a pay-phone and telephoned the police. I said, "This is the IRA – we have planted a time-bomb in ————————'s boutique in Oxford Street and you have forty-five minutes to clear the area before it explodes." I dropped the handset of the phone and then rang again one minute later to make sure the message had been received. I did not wait to hear if the policeman who answered my call had any questions.

We walked along Oxford Street for some distance and looked to where the police should soon arrive to begin clearing the area. After ten or more minutes, there had still been no police activity, and I began to get a little concerned. The time-bomb we had planted was relatively small, but in the confines of the basement shop which would contain the explosion, the damage would be considerable, and anyone in there would be killed.

Once more, as in the case of the government building in Derry almost two years earlier, the police were not responding to two phone calls giving a warning of the bomb. It occurred to me that they could be receiving scores or hundreds of hoax warning calls every day in a city the size of London. I went to another phone and called the police for the third time in something of a panic. I cursed myself for not having gotten the phone number of the shop – as a last resort I could have called it directly with the warning.

There was nothing more I could do. The bomb was timed to go off in less than five minutes, and the telephone warnings to the police had failed. I left with the girl and returned to the apartment on the tube. I switched on LBC to learn that there had been a small explosion in a shop in Oxford Street and bomb squad officers were now checking the area. No-one had been injured. I could not believe it!

I had to wait some hours for clarification, but when it came it was mysterious – only the detonator of the device had exploded. The four-ounce packets of gelatin had failed to detonate. I just couldn't understand it – all of the other bombs had detonated... Once more, a total disaster had been avoided by a freak accident.

I concluded that I could no longer trust the police and that I should in future direct warning calls to the Press Association, and offer a code word so that my real bomb warnings could be differentiated from hoax calls. I rang the P.A. twice and declared that I was speaking on behalf of the IRA, and that a code word for future bomb warnings would be "Double X". Thereafter, the warning calls were always taken seriously.

My money ran out well before anyone thought it would, and a courier was late bringing more. I had been to the Pakistani restaurant a couple of times and the young waiter and I were by now quite friendly. He always brought my half-bottle of Sauternes. When the courier arrived with money and some new orders, I complained bitterly to him that I had been penniless for nearly a week, that there was no food in the fridge, that I had practically starved and that it was just not good enough. I told him that I had had no social life, apart from my weekly cinema visits.

The courier guiltily offered to take me out for a meal. I accepted, and suggested the quiet Pakistani restaurant. We got there and were seated at table, when my young Pakistani waiter friend, intent on making an impact on my guest, swirled over in his white short coat and bow-tie and held up a bottle of Sauternes to the words, "Your usual wine, Sir?" My courier looked on in amazement as I tried to explain. Everywhere I went in Ireland after this, in circles where I was known, I heard the refrain, "Your usual wine, Sir?"

Looking back from Christmas 1973, the letter bombs had had amazing success – one got into 10 Downing Street, but had failed to explode and had lain unnoticed in a waste paper bin for twenty-four hours before a secretary had realized what it was; another had blown up the Brigadier; above all, the Bloody Sunday Home Secretary, Reginald Maudling, had been blown up at his country home; the Stock Exchange, the Bank of England and a British Embassy had been the site of explosions. The last three explosions had involved persons to whom the letter bombs were not addressed, secretaries and a security man. I had not intended to injure these people, and regretted that the markings on the envelopes, which ranged from Private and Confidential to Official Stamps and Government envelopes, had not prevented them from being opened. A police bomb disposal officer had also been injured trying to defuse a letter bomb. In separate incidents, some postal workers were injured handling devices, which prompted industrial action. I took no joy or pleasure from the fact of their injuries. In these operations I had failed to get the letter bombs to the targets. I began to wonder if the devices were too hazardous to innocent persons whose job it might be to deal with the addressee's mail.

London had been tremendously disrupted by this one-man campaign. Business and government mail and communications had been slowed beyond belief. Huge signs were erected outside tube stations warning morning commuters against suspicious mail. Hoax bomb warnings were being phoned in by all and sundry. The IRA was exceedingly pleased that all this international publicity and disruption of London had been achieved for a few pounds of explosives, less than a thousand pounds in cash, a single volunteer, and not a single arrest.

Back in Dublin, I was told to wait at a safe house because the Chief of Staff wished to see me very briefly. I waited for hours one evening, until the family began to think that I was exaggerating my own importance with my story that I was waiting for the C.S. He did arrive, but, in keeping with his life on the move, stayed in the hallway for less than a minute where he shook my hand warmly and said, "A good job well done!" With that he was whisked out to his car and taken off to God knows where. I was happy that he appreciated the risks I had taken and the impact I had been able to make on London.

The G.H.Q. person for whom I was operating in England was arrested back in Ireland, and when I returned to find out who my new contact person was, I did not like the temporary replacement, primarily because he had never operated and didn't know what he was talking about. Operators never liked to take orders from armchair generals, and I was no exception. I did not like his casual attitude to risks that might be taken with civilian lives in London. I told him that I was Derry Brigade trained, and would not deviate from my belief that risks were to be absolutely minimized. I had a huge row with him, and told him I was not going back to London. He threatened to have me court martialed, and I walked out on him.

I was now finished with London bombings, and had to find a new placement, particularly until the threat of court martial was lifted. I first of all made for a Border unit where I was known and trusted. They kept me busy on a landmine operation against a British Army armored vehicle. I meanwhile mentioned my situation to various persons who were powerful enough to see that no inappropriate action was taken against me over the argument about London. The temporary replacement who had fallen out with me was replaced soon after.

I knew that explosives detonated in London reaped a far greater harvest than a hundred times the amount used in Northern Ireland, but, despite this, and the arguments about the injustice of making young, expendable soldiers pay with their lives for centuries of British interference in Ireland, I fell back into the rut of pitting my wits and my devices against that same Army, largely because it was there.

And so, one evening on the Northern side of the Border between Northern Ireland and the Irish Republic, I watched an amazing sight by moonlight. Six men were working fast to dig a huge hole in a dirt road. When they were satisfied with its dimensions, a large tipper-truck backed up and dumped a vast amount of explosive into the hole, whereupon I walked up and put in a detonating charge of high explosive. I moved back, and the men smoothed over the road surface, taking care to remove all of the excess earth. They got out, and I was left alone with a guide. I returned to the buried bomb and attached an electronic receiver to it, with an almost invisible aerial, which would detonate the bomb at my signal.

It was unnerving to stand on what must have been a bomb of some six hundred or more pounds, knowing that if it exploded prematurely, I was not going to know much about it... I was then shown to a vantage point almost level with the site of the landmine, and left there with a thermos flask of tea and a couple of boiled eggs which warmed my hands in my pockets. I was in a hide constructed of bits of bush and hedge which was good enough to camouflage me in full daylight. It got very cold in the middle of the night, indeed, too cold for me. In the bright moonlight, I could see a small barn nearby and I went over to it. I shall never forget the relative heat of the air in the barn where, using my emergency flashlight, I counted eight cows. I clambered up on bales of hay and, warmed, fell asleep.

I was awake and functioning when the sun came up, giving a beautiful yellow light to the grass and trees nearby. For fifteen minutes, I checked the landscape with binoculars for signs of Army activity before I felt secure enough to return to my hide, which, by daylight, seemed too close to the mine for my liking. I was expecting an armored car to trundle along the road before long and I was going to attempt to blow it to smithereens, after which I was supposed to crawl up the hillock behind me, along a little stream whose carved course would cover me. I was then to be picked up and driven in a direction opposite to that which the Army expected – the Army was under the useful impression that operators headed for the Border.

As I sat in the hide, I heard the drone of a helicopter in the far distance, and watched it approach above the very road which was mined. This was the Army's morning visual search for booby traps, and I hoped that this one was going to be missed. The chopper passed near me, and I almost thought it spotted me, but it flew on. It occurred to me that it was so low in flight that the landmine could probably have taken it down. Nothing happened for a few hours, and then, after a few moments of inattention, I glanced at the road to find that an armored car was already parked near the mine. It must have freewheeled down the road for some time, because the high-pitched whine of the Rolls Royce engines was normally audible for a very long distance, and I had heard nothing. I grabbed my transmitter, put my finger on the button and watched through my binoculars, but saw no signs of movement.

I began to think that perhaps the helicopter had spotted something different on the road surface and that the armored car was checking it out, which meant that this mine might soon be discovered and defused. I had to decide what to do about it, but had little to go on apart from what I could see. If the Army thought there might be a mine somewhere, it was certainly keeping watch for the button-presser also, but the fact that the helicopter had not returned to give cover inclined me to the view that my suspicions were groundless. The armored car was parked there for some other reason. It was too far from the mine to be vulnerable. I waited.

The engines then started up and revved. It seemed to move towards the mine and I pressed the button. A powerful shock wave hit me in the chest, the earth met the sky in an instant, and a massive roar rumbled around the countryside. I was up and moving towards the channel of the stream before the roar subsided. As I leapt a small fence into the stream, the cracks of high velocity rifles cut the air by me, and I went up the hillock on my hands and knees, tearing my jeans at the knees, and cutting my hands. Fire was definitely being directed at me, but from where? When I reached the top of the hillock, and just before I dodged out of sight of the gunmen, I looked back from behind a tree and clearly saw the black devastation of the countryside, and what looked like a good number of soldiers working towards me – the armored car must have dropped off a patrol before I spotted it, and the patrol had seen me.

I hurried to where my driver was waiting anxiously. He told me he'd never heard an explosion like it – neither had I! I was wondering if the armored car had been damaged at all – it was not easy to inflict a wound on an armored car. We got out of the area no problem, helped by the fact that all the security was thrown up around the border, not in the other direction.

It was a bad idea to detonate a bomb on a Saturday evening. It was too late to be reported in most Sunday newspapers, got a minor paragraph in one, and was forgotten about on Monday. The two-ounces in London theory was certainly proven by this six-hundred pounder in Northern Ireland...

I got caught up in country operations for a time. A young man had been killed attempting to plant what should have been a quite safe radio-controlled bomb on a bridge checkpoint used by the Army in Tyrone. Someone who was interested in finding out how such mistakes occurred, asked me to try to put another similar device into the same Army checkpoint. I said I would give it a go. The Army was known to have mobile radio devices constantly "sweeping" country areas with signals in an attempt to detonate radio-controlled bombs before the IRA could do so. The IRA was on the brink of developing a system that could not be sweep-detonated. The premature explosion on the bridge was problematic.

I looked at the Army checkpoint from a distance. It seemed impregnable. The Irish Republic's police had a permanent checkpoint on the Southern side of the Border in full view of the British one, and sufficient to prevent any attack originating on the Southern side. I had no intention of attacking from the South.

I was very surprised to notice that the British Army left their checkpoint for a short time every evening, at the changing of the guard. The sandbag post was vacant for less than ten minutes, so this was obviously the time to plant a bomb. I discussed the problem with the unit operating in Tyrone, and they suggested hijacking a very large lorry, driving it from the North to the Army checkpoint, stalling it just beyond the checkpoint, blocking the view of the Southern police, at which point I would dart from the rear of the lorry into the sandbag post to remove sandbags and plant my radio-controlled bomb.

The operation worked as described and I had a hair-raising time getting the bomb into the sandbag post, while the Southern police craned their necks to see why this huge lorry was stalled, and while the British Army made ready to return to the checkpoint which they should never have left. I got the device in, raised the little aerial and jumped back into the lorry, which was then driven towards the Southern police, who asked about the engine problem, had a look into the lorry, and let us pass.

I then travelled North again, and took up position on a little hill which let me view the British checkpoint. I readied myself to fire the bomb when the soldiers entered the post, but before that, another van passed, revved its engine for some reason or other. There was a flash, sandbags hit the sky, then a boom rolled over the area. When I could see through the smoke, the van had been blown some distance, the checkpoint was gone, the Irish police were taking cover and once more it had been proven that there was something problematic about that bridge. I got out before helicopters discovered my position, still unsure about the cause of these premature explosions. No-one had been killed in this one, but if the Army had arrived before the van, soldiers would certainly have died.

In early 1974 at the age of 19, I asked the Derry Brigade to take me back. There was at least one voice raised against having me operate again in Derry, because it was thought that if the British Army and intelligence services thought that I was around, they would tear Derry apart to find me. There was no doubt that an IRA man who sent a two-ounce letter bomb into 10 Downing Street was higher on the wanted list than anyone else who had merely killed a few Brits in Northern Ireland. That was the way it was, (as the police graphically told me when they finally arrested me over a year later).

I was finally given permission to enter Derry, but was left sitting ignominiously in a house across the river Foyle in the Waterside for some weeks while the debate went on about my acceptability. I was assured that I would be told if any operations were going to occur near me, so that I might take precautions against arrest in follow-up operations by the British Army and police. As I sat late one afternoon in my safe house, waiting for the call that never came, there was a huge explosion only a street or two away. As it echoed across the city, I told my startled hosts that I had obviously not been told about every operation that was going on, and was now in dire danger of being arrested when the Army and police swooped in response to whatever the explosion had hit. I decided that I had had enough of sitting around in the Waterside, and immediately left the house and walked to Craigavon Bridge to cross the Foyle to the Derry city centre side and the Bogside ghetto. The bridge had a permanent Army checkpoint at this time through which pedestrians were often allowed to walk unhindered, presumably because wanted IRA men were not expected to cross in broad daylight. I hurried across the bridge before the response to the explosion had been fully organized, and made it through the checkpoint without incident.

It turned out that the blast had been a booby trap aimed at the Army, but civilians had stumbled upon it and had been seriously injured. I went straight to a safe house in the Bogside from which I sent word to the IRA Brigade Staff that I had arrived, was angry about the explosion, and felt aggrieved by the Derry Brigade's treatment of me.

The Brigade Staff was short of an explosives' officer at this time, following the arrest and imprisonment of the previous incumbent. It was not the kind of position for which there was a lot of competition, and I was duly elected to it. I was barely nineteen years old and was the youngest member of the Brigade Staff, but a veteran of operations. However, when the Brigade was taking collective decisions, my opinion might or might not be sought. I went along with this to some degree, making it clear that I really wanted to operate, not to get involved in overall Brigade business, which might include talking to Community Associations, Churchmen, politicians and other boring bureaucratic activity like that...

I was now responsible for any and every explosive device made and used in the Derry Brigade area. I should have a say in the training and qualification of Battalion and Company explosives' officers, and in the general safety precautions in use by the Brigade not only for its own volunteers, but also for the population at large. I could also instigate particular attacks by coming up with ideas, or I could add my support to the ideas of others. In fact, I could write my own job description. While I was responsible overall for explosives, other members of the staff could direct that certain things should happen and I would have to go along with it. I was not in sole control.

I had to make a mark to prove that I was still very much operational in Derry terms. I was asked to become involved in an incendiary attack on a resort town, and I reluctantly agreed. I did not like operating in areas where I did not feel familiar or competent, but I had to do it. I made up a large number of devices and on the day, had them ready on the floor carpet of a house in the Waterside, ready for the people to collect and take by car to the resort, where they would plant them in shops. I had decided to take the same risks as those volunteers planting the devices, and chose my own target where I intended to put several fire-bombs.

I was arming a couple of devices for the first of the people who arrived to collect the electronically-ignited incendiaries, when the ignition part of one flared up on the carpet. I kept the ignition parts out of the incendiaries until I had armed them and had seen that they were safe, then I inserted them into the incendiary material. It was just as well in this case. I was quite embarrassed by my mistake, by the flame, by the small hole in the carpet, by the girl's obvious fright. I quickly recovered, though, and said to her, "See? This is my fail-safe method of checking for faulty devices, and it worked and weeded out this one. The rest are absolutely fine as you can see for yourself." She relaxed completely. I noticed that I had forgotten to set the timer when I had joined the two wires, so the circuit had been completed and the ignition part had gone off. That was my first mistake, but I had gotten over it.

When everyone had assembled to collect the incendiaries, someone made the point that the Ulster Defense Association, the big Protestant paramilitary, had called for a strike in Protestant areas of Northern Ireland under the title of the Ulster Workers' Council. This meant that most shops and entertainments would be closed in Protestant towns or areas of those towns. However, the seaside resort we were going to try to hit was not the sort of place to give much credence to the mostly Belfast-based UDA, and the Commander who had pushed for this operation was not going to be put off by anything so inconsequential.

We drove off at five minute intervals in our various cars, astonished to find that trees had been felled along the main road at some points by UDA sympathizers. The police waved us past these partial obstructions, pleased that we were people who had not obeyed the UDA instruction to strike. On arrival in the seaside resort, we found that, as I'd guessed, most premises were open for business. We set about our respective tasks and I made it back to the car within forty-five minutes. We decided to set off for Derry immediately, but even before we got out of the car-park, a fire engine sirened past us, followed by another. They went straight to where I'd planted my devices, and began to play hoses in the upper windows of the building. I couldn't believe it, since the timers on the devices should not have ignited them until during the night. A crowd gathered to view the fire.

We drove off before the police could set up checkpoints in the small town, and took a roundabout way back to Derry, because there were sure to be roadblocks on the main road. We got home to learn that some of our comrades had been arrested by the police while trying to plant incendiaries. It had not been a very good day. The attack was hardly mentioned on the news.

I had to get myself organized into my Brigade role, which meant laying off operations for a while. I tried to make fundamental changes to the way the Brigade used explosives, to make their use safer for both the IRA people using them, and for the civilian population who had to live and work around the IRA campaign. I sought to get all of the individual explosives' officers, whether from the companies or battalions, into a pool over which I could exercise control, producing better training and improved safety standards. Pooling them would make higher quality operatives available to any unit or area, whereas before, the unit would have to rely on its own somewhat isolated explosives' officer.

My first priority was to get a number of ultra-safe billets, or safe houses, so that I would always have somewhere secure to rest up, sleep, or spend periods of inactivity, if there were any. I managed this quickly, mainly by looking at areas I knew the Army did not expect to find bitter Republican resistance or views, and then gathering information on families who lived there who would in fact have Republican sympathies. I would then whittle these down to a couple of virtual certainties, and call to talk to the parents and ask them straight out if they would like to keep a wanted IRA man by night. There was a fairly limited financial support towards the meals and beverages they might serve to a "guest", amounting to perhaps a large grocery basket per week. I met some fine people who were prepared to risk keeping me, even after I told them that I was wanted for London bombings, and still retain their friendship.

I then needed to find houses, flats or apartments which I could use for making and storing explosives and related equipment, where the Army and police didn't expect them to be, and where people coming and going to or from them might be less conspicuous. I eventually got a number of them, and was able to move in my equipment and begin construction of devices, storage of same, training and operations.

I had to run training camps for the experienced and for the new explosives' people, which took a lot of time. It was possible to run a training camp in a house in Derry over a weekend, or even for three days. The days of taking people to remote parts of Tyrone, Antrim, Derry or Donegal were almost gone.

In the eight or nine months between my return to Derry as Brigade Explosives' Officer and the onset of the IRA ceasefire between December '74 and mid-75, I worked full-time on the most efficient and lethal IRA campaign I had ever experienced in Derry. The Brigade Staff was extremely competent and had the respect and trust not only of the IRA volunteers, but of the great majority of the community in the ghettos, who knew very well the people who made up the IRA in Derry.

I spent hours making explosive and incendiary devices in my favorite bolt-hole, a flat in a trouble-free part of Derry. There were periods when I stayed up all night making incendiaries, and other occasions when I had to tailor-make explosives to fit a particular operation.

Once or twice I was defeated by the IRA's own code allied to the even stronger spirit of Derry women. For instance, it came to my attention that a Catholic man living in the ghetto had a key to a government building, and that he returned to his home for lunch, a period when we could take the key from him at gunpoint, and go and incendiarize or bomb the building. This was the idea, at any rate, but I hadn't planned for every eventuality. I wanted to work with the unit most concerned with executing this job, and I took it upon myself to get the key from the man. On the appointed day, when the incendiary bombs were ready and waiting to go into the government building, I went to the man's home at lunchtime along with one of the unit lads. We called at the front door, and were met by the man's wife. I asked if I might see him about a private matter, and she invited us into their small home and let us wait in the front sitting-room. Her husband came in and greeted us. He was not a young man, nor did he look entirely well. There was the noise of children in the kitchen, obviously having lunch.

I addressed the man in a low voice, telling him that I was from the IRA, and that I had come to take his key to the government building. I said that he should not try to resist and that we wanted to avoid any unpleasantness.

The man looked even more pale when I'd finished speaking. He replied that his health was bad and that his religious conscience would never allow him to hand over the key.

I told him that I was now his conscience, that my gun absolved him from moral guilt, and that I wanted the key.

At this point, his wife, who must have wondered what two lads had to do with her husband, came into the room, saw her husband looking very pale, and asked what was going on.

Our friend, having played the illness and the religious cards, now played the trump card – instead of trying to keep his wife out of this men's business, he involved her straightaway. With an uncanny instinct for a way out, he told her that we were from the IRA and were demanding the key to his building. He passed it to her, and, as I looked on with that sinking feeling, she popped it down the open neck of her lace blouse and presumably into her bra... I knew that there was nothing to be done, that the IRA's intent had been defeated by this woman's action. No Derry IRA volunteer could interfere with a Bogside woman.

She stated that I was definitely not getting the key, that hers was a Catholic family and wanted no part of violence. I still had an argument left in me and responded that thirteen Catholic people wanted nothing to do with violence on a Civil Rights march in this very street, but were murdered by British Army paratroopers. I said I wanted nothing to do with violence, but that freedom of choice often had to be fought for.

She offered tea and biscuits, the final ignominy. I went back to Brigade to tell them that a woman had popped one of our biggest jobs down her blouse. Brigade agreed that there had been no alternative but to call it off.

We wanted to hit Victoria police barracks, the headquarters of the R.U.C. in Derry, but it was difficult. There was, however, an outfitters next door to the police station, called, ironically enough, Crooks. It struck me that if we fire-bombed it properly, the resultant heat and structural damage would roast the police station next door. I set about making the very best miniature incendiaries and had a variety of them put into a dump (an IRA quartermaster's store) in Thundering Down, with a note attached to them forbidding anyone else taking or using them and explaining that they were for a special job. It was not unknown for one unit to appropriate another's material.

I was both horrified and amused to learn that the dump had been raided and all my special incendiaries and my note had been captured. I wondered what the police and Army would make of my note, (and found out a year later when I was arrested). I made some more special incendiaries incorporating magnesium and lighter fuel, and tested the tiny watch-timers until I was sure they worked. I found volunteers for placing the incendiaries in Crooks just before closing time and suggested various sites. They were set to ignite between three and four a.m.

My favorite flat was set on a hill overlooking the city and I arranged with the person who kept it to have a rare steak dinner by the big window at three a.m. with a bottle of Sauternes to view what I hoped would be a big blaze. We were eating and sipping and looking down across the dark city when I noticed an orange glow around Crooks' roof. The glow had become a bright blaze before fire engines whined through the streets toward the fire. They were way too late. I had radios tuned to the fire brigade and Army frequencies and we listened to their commentaries as the blaze gutted the building and damaged the police station next door, blistering paint on vehicles parked in the police yard. I slept the sleep of the just that night, happy that I had clocked up another action against the forces which might at any time shoot me dead on the street.

The evening that the British Army cornered me and should have captured me happened as follows: I wanted to booby trap an empty garage in the Bogside and then use the police Confidential Telephone, a freefone for informers, to report suspicious activity around it in the hope that the Army would raid it. I got all my gadgetry together and went to the garage to make and plant as many individual booby traps in it as it would physically hold, including a copy of "Who's Who" bearing an anti-handling device. This was going to take a few hours and I needed someone to hold the doors closed from the inside, because they opened outwards and the bolt was on the outside. A young volunteer asked to be allowed to do it, and I agreed and took him along. I was working by torchlight and was about two hours into my tasks and surrounded by explosives, detonators and batteries when the lad holding the doors whispered in a panic, "The Brits are outside!"

I immediately thought that an informer had betrayed us, and I guessed that there was no way the Brits were going to take me alive if they captured me red-handed in the act of planting booby traps. I went to the crack between the doors and looked out into the darkness to see Army vehicles revving their engines and disgorging soldiers a matter of feet away from us. But instead of charging at the garage doors or shooting through them, they set up a vehicle checkpoint and even backed one Army troop carrier up the lane until the rear of the vehicle was about three feet from where we were behind our doors.

I couldn't believe that they were this close and weren't going to find us. We held our breaths for what seemed like hours, fearing that the loud thumping of our hearts must be audible to the troops mounting guard in the adjacent darkness. But no, an order was shouted, the vehicles revved and pulled away, and we were left to recover and I to finish my work. That had been a very close call. A sharp-eyed soldier might have noticed that the lock securing the doors on the outside was undone, that the doors were open, and that it might have been a good idea to check the garage before parking a troop carrier beside it. Fortunately, there was no sharp-eyed soldier that evening.

In due course, the Confidential Telephone was used to inform the police and army that suspicious activity had been noticed at the garage. The Army came in to raid it, but did so very carefully, obviously expecting a surprise or two. They sent in a robot device and up went the "Who's Who", after which they let the robot take the place apart.

I got into a row with a Catholic family nearby, who were very kind to me while I was on the run. One of the daughters, aided by one of her religious friends, objected to the explosions in the garage and had no doubt that I was responsible. They questioned the value of using violence in a good cause, because of the violations of human rights which inevitably followed. Should I, they argued, lower myself to the level of the British paratroopers on Bloody Sunday in setting out to kill human beings for whatever reason? Her brother, separately, wondered aloud what he would have done if he'd known in advance that I was planting the devices; would he, he mused, have had the ability to keep silent and let the soldiers enter the garage, or would he have felt compelled by his conscience to inform them by telephone about the danger?

I answered both arguments the same way, saying that it was a perennial Irish problem to so problematize freedom struggle, or Independence warfare, as to make it impossible. If a subject people were always to put religious conscience and moral objections before force of arms as the avenue to freedom, then old Imperialist oppressors need not worry about expansion of their unjust conquests – they would just invade and conquer and let religious conscience, aided and abetted by that oldest friend of Imperialism, the Catholic Church, consolidate their unjust gain.

I asked them who had the greater moral right to bear arms in Ireland – an Irishman fighting for Irish freedom, or a foreign soldier bent on shoring up an illegal, immoral conquest? What morality had the British to convince them that their unjust treatment of Ireland and the Irish for eight hundred years was just and proper? What view of human rights in Britain supported the occupation of the territory of a neighboring country, the use of internment without trial and torture, the murders of innocent civil rights' marchers, and the wholesale terrorization of the Republican community which wanted to be free of British rule?

All of us however nursed an unhappiness about the present state of affairs, one believing that to change it required force, the other believing that the Christian doctrine of pacifism precluded this. I did not like such criticism coming from people I expected to condone my activity. For all my debating skill, I was not so sure that I was right about violence.

I was walking out from the Bogside one night to my flat when two Military Policemen, in their distinctive uniforms and red-topped hats, stopped me on Francis Street to question me. I always anticipated being stopped and had a good excuse ready every time. On this occasion, I was carrying a six-pack of beer and gave them the line that I was going to a party on Northland Road. I showed them my student I.D. and they let me go, and I wondered why these two heroes felt that they could mount a lone checkpoint so close to the Bogside without fear of attack. They were crazy.

I was sufficiently concerned about my own safety and that of the people who worked with me to want to know if any operations were planned for areas where I had flats containing explosives and other materials. I kept asking the Director of Operations to tell me. When I reached the flat that evening, I looked out the window to see two more Military Policemen walking across waste ground nearby. They may have been the same two who stopped me, or they may have been two others. Sometimes some bright spark in Army headquarters, who knew nothing of the reality on the ground, gave orders that Military Policemen should have a greater profile, but seemingly without adequate defense.

I had hardly replaced the curtains and walked to the kitchen, when there was a fierce burst of shots very close by, followed by the sound of a car screeching away. I knew immediately that the two MPs had been shot, and I trembled at what the Army response would be. There was no way that I could get out of the area now. I would have to sit tight and hope that there would not be a house-to-house search operation. If there was, I would be caught in a flat loaded with explosives and gadgetry.

The British Army arrived on the scene in force after about five minutes, quickly followed by the second fiddle, the Royal Ulster Constabulary. I took only one look out the window, and the place was crawling with armed soldiers. A radio news bulletin reported that two Military Police soldiers had been shot in the head at close range, and that two revolvers had been found nearby. There was no house-to-house search and eventually the Army retreated back to barracks, with the police in tow. My complaint about not being told of the operation was diluted by the fact that there had been no search, and no direct danger to me or to any of my explosives. As for the two Military Policemen, I had no time to agonize over their fate, since a similar fate possibly awaited me. They were on military duty in a country not their own, and had been prepared to risk their lives – they had lost.

A Catholic relation of mine, with whom I often stayed, talked to me about religious matters and harried me about the Sacrament of Confession. If I were day and daily living with the likelihood of losing my life either at the hands of the British Army or in an accidental explosion, could I not, she argued, at least make use of the confessional, even if I only had a chat with the priest? Could I not discuss with him the fact that I did not think my struggle against the British Army was sinful?

I thought the world of this relation who had been so good to me, and I agreed to go with her on her next trip to the Cathedral where I had sung as a choirboy for some years, St. Eugene's, virtually at the top of Clarendon Street.

One Saturday evening when she was going to be shriven, I accompanied her and entered the whispering silence of St. Eugene's marbled, tiled otherworld. I sat in the pew by a confessional, waited for my turn, and after my relation had been in and had told the priest that I was coming next, I entered the box, closed the squeaky door and faced the wire grille. After a few minutes, it slid open and the priest said, "In the name of the Father, Son and Holy Spirit, Amen. May the Lord be in your heart and on your lips that you may humbly confess your sins."

I told him I was in the IRA, and that I was interested in discussing the morality of violence in liberation struggle. He asked me if I'd committed any acts of violence. I replied that I had been fighting the Brits using methods and material identical to theirs, but without pay. He wanted to know if I'd killed anyone. I told him I'd tried often to kill the enemy, before it killed me. He was short and sharp – was I there to confess my sins? I told him I was there to discuss the morality of violence in liberation struggle.

"I cannot help you there. The Church, through the Holy Father, and the Bishops, and I, as your priest, tell you that murder and violence are sinful and always wrong."

"What about Wars of Independence, and Liberation Struggle? What about unjust and immoral occupation and oppression of one country by its stronger, bullying neighbor? Is the status quo always the lesser of two evils, and the greater evil armed resistance?"

"I cannot help you. You may come back when you have sins to confess."

I left the confessional irritated and angry with myself for having gotten into the situation at all. My relation was sitting in a nearby pew with shining eyes and a saintly mien, eager to learn of my confession and repentance. She asked, "Well, was it okay?"

"It was fine," I replied, "just fine." She, at least, was happy, under the impression that if I was murdered by the Brits now, or killed in action against them, or blown up by my own bomb, I had secured a visa assuring me of entry to heaven, or, at the very least, purgatory. The Roman Catholic Church in Ireland has always taught the Irish that it is more important to gain such visas than National Freedom and Independence.

A feminist breeze blew momentarily across the Derry Brigade at this time. I was asked if I would train a number of young women in the arts and crafts of explosives, women who were more used to secondary roles as in the transport and dumping (storing) of materials and weapons. I agreed immediately, seeing all kinds of opportunities for them to use such talents in situations where men would arouse suspicion. I arranged a weekend training camp in a most scenic and remote part of the coast for the first young women I had ever had the opportunity to train. We were located in a forgotten farmhouse near sheer cliffs and a wild and restless sea. These women were equal to any male trainees I had taught, and were ready on the final morning to prime and set the timers on their own small bombs. They were going to plant these on the seashore, a "hands-on" and very real experience I thought people should have before they operated in cities.

I had been given small bags of the IRA's own explosive, made from benzene and fertilizer, which I had only ever used as a primer to set off much larger bombs of "mix" (a lower grade home-made bulk explosive), and so I didn't know the power of the actual benzene material itself. I didn't rate it very highly, since I preferred commercial and plastic explosives. I thought the small bags of benzene which I gave them with detonators and detonating cord, and which I wanted them to use in the construction of their first real bombs, would not make very much noise on the seashore, as they exploded one after the other, at five minute intervals.

So, between five and six a.m., I stood on the seashore beside each woman as she made, timed and primed her device. There were eight in all, and the nine of us then retired to a nearby cliff top to view the small puffs of smoke and gentle pops which I expected. If any device failed to explode, I would have to either defuse it or blow it up myself. The group was very excited when the first bomb was due to explode, and the seconds ticked away on my watch. All of a sudden, there was a deafening BOOM! Sand and sky merged. We all fell backwards on our asses. The incredible sound echoed around the townland on this previously peaceful Sunday morning, waking every living being within miles. We ran back to the farmhouse to evacuate it of incriminating material and to get into the cars and out of the area before roadblocks were set up. I sent the women off in separate cars, and told my driver to wait for me. I put every piece of training equipment in a bag with what remaining explosive I had, and attached a detonator and safety fuse to it, which I lit and then tossed into the sea from the clifftop. The bag sank, and was blown to smithereens thirty seconds later deep under water, without a BOOM! to endanger us. However, as I ran to my car to make my own escape, bomb number two exploded in an equally deafening thunder.

It was now imperative to put as much distance as possible between us and the exploding beach, before the roads were crawling with police. We were careering along the road when we clearly heard bomb number three as its detonation passed overhead and onward to stir up a hornets' nest of activity into which I was sure we were going to drive. The local people, who'd found us the training camp facilities and accepted my assurance that any explosions would be small ones, barely audible above the cliffs and seashore, would have been blown out of bed by the first, and blown into a panic by the other seven... and my reputation would be seriously damaged.

I thought ahead to my appearance in court, charged with blowing up a public beach eight times, and to my being the laughing-stock of the IRA and the prisons... We were almost out of danger when a fast unmarked car passed us and forced us to stop. A police car appeared behind us. Armed men in plainclothes approached and said, "Would you mind stepping out of the car, please?"

"What for?"

"Just routine. Step out of the car please."

"Certainly." We got out and stepped back from the car, and one of the plainclothes ordered the uniforms to search the car minutely. He was certain that they were going to find explosives, so certain, in fact, that he omitted to search me or the driver at that point. As I stood by the ditch while the car was taken apart by four uniformed officers, I put my hand into the pocket of my green Barbour jacket to find it crammed with electric detonators, pieces of detonating cord, and other incriminating material... I checked the other pocket and found the same... I couldn't believe that in the panic at the seashore I had forgotten to search my own pockets and was now liable to be arrested for such stupidity! What should I do? We were being watched closely by the plainclothes, but our own visible confidence up to now had inclined them to the view that we would not be carrying anything. I was sorely tempted to try to throw or drop the contents of my pockets into the ditch behind me, but worried that I might be caught. There was the slimmest possibility that we were not going to be searched at all. I gambled.

After a lengthy examination of the car, it became obvious that there was nothing in it. The plainclothes were deeply disappointed. My driver still showed supreme confidence, unaware that I was loaded with gadgetry.

"Sorry to bother you. You may proceed."

I couldn't believe it. I got in the car, still expecting to be told to empty my pockets and stand for a body search, but we drove off unmolested. After putting a considerable distance between us and the cops, I produced a handful of detonators to the driver's view...

The backdrop to all these incidents was one of a confident and successful IRA campaign in Derry with a great deal of visible and invisible support from the community. The high degree of organization and abundant volunteers for the campaign gave us a sense of supremacy over the fumbling foreign Army and the timid police behind it. On another occasion, one of the Bogside units said that they had noticed that the Army left one of its checkpoints temporarily at about 8am every morning in the city centre, probably because it was surrounded by the general security in the shopping areas anyway. This unit wanted to place a smallish explosive device under a table or chair in the sandbag observation post while the soldiers were away, timed to explode when they returned.

I supplied a stick of high explosives with a miniature timer, set with the delay they had requested. On the morning, as I lay in bed in one of my flats, I heard a loud explosion at the appropriate time. The Army radio frequency reported in something of a panic that the observation post had been blown-up from the inside, while the troops were about to enter it. It was highly embarrassing for the British Army, and a sign of IRA confidence, that bombs could be placed in the very Army checkpoints which were aimed at preventing bombs getting into the city centre...

I got a small, high explosive device right against the front desk of Victoria Police Barracks one Saturday afternoon, where it exploded without warning causing damage not only to the fabric, but to the morale of the police. The Brigade Staff were listening to the Army and police radio frequencies before, during and after the explosion, and heard Army comments on the abysmal security which the police maintained over their own headquarters. The police had to ignominiously evacuate Victoria Barracks while Army bomb disposal experts checked the building for other devices... How could the police guarantee security for anywhere else, when their city headquarters was insecure? All in all, we were running rings around the Army and police in Derry.

CHAPTER 6

Breach of The Ceasefire

In the autumn of 1974, it was mentioned at a Brigade meeting that there was some feeling that the campaign required an opportunity through which to turn the military successes into political progress. It was said that some people were suggesting that a ceasefire might be a possibility and that the British Government might be willing to enter into negotiations to bring about an agreement to end the hostilities.

We had been meeting with elected politicians for some time for very informal talks. I was staying with a family which had strong political affiliations, and, at a time when other members of the Brigade Staff needed somewhere to stay, they stayed with this family, while I moved out to one of my flats. As a result, various informal talks occurred at this house between public representatives and the IRA Brigade Staff.

Later, at another Brigade meeting, it was put to us that there was a very strong chance that there would be a ceasefire agreement between the British Government and Army on the one side, and the IRA on the other. We were asked what we individually thought about the process that might bring it about.

This matter was the subject of regular discussion from that point on, and sometimes caused bitter disagreement. Not everyone thought that the way forward with the British Government was a cessation of the military campaign, believing that the British would exploit any ceasefire to cause division in the ranks of the Republican Movement, to catch up on intelligence gathering and informer recruitment, and to give the impression to the public at home and abroad that a victory of sorts had been achieved over the IRA. This argument was backed up with the details of the immense suffering which the Nationalist and Republican community had borne to date, and of the deaths and sacrifice of many IRA volunteers – how could all of this be traded for an end to the campaign, and no British declaration of intent to withdraw from Ireland? Was this not a likeness of the infamous Treaty which the Old IRA had signed with the British Government in 1921, which had resulted in over half a million Irish Catholics being trapped against their will in second-class citizenship in the Protestant, pro-British state of Northern Ireland, causing all of this trouble fifty years on?

Those giving their support to the ceasefire process argued that it was absolutely necessary for all of the above reasons to claw back some political progress from the horror, to translate all of that suffering into some realistic deal with the British. They wanted to bring to an end the incredible lifestyle of the IRA people at the time, which meant for those who were wanted and "on the run", that married men rarely saw their wives or children, had given up their careers or small businesses, were in some debt, and could not offer any prospect of improvement to their families. For single men like me, it meant not being able to finish an education or get a job or job-related experience, that romantic relationships were difficult to establish or maintain, and that family and social relations were put under incredible strain.

It meant for everyone the possibility of an instantaneous death at the hands of the terrorist murderers of the SAS or similar British death squads, sometimes working in collusion with Protestant paramilitaries, or else internment without trial, or very long periods of imprisonment. Being full-time operators for the IRA was really a mode of life that was acceptable for a limited period only. Therefore, the argument went, it was necessary to deal, and to get the best deal. After all, the Armed Struggle could be resurrected at a later date if necessary. This is where the argument stumbled. Those suggesting this knew full well that it was easier by far to stop a campaign, than to try to restart it when everyone had had a taste of peace and home life.

Some individuals were extremely angry about even the mention of a ceasefire possibility, regarding it as treasonable talk, and a traitorous sellout of everything for which their comrades had fought and died.

It was against this background that the Big Push began to be talked about. If a military or paramilitary organization were going into talks about a temporary or permanent ceasefire, it followed that it would want to be seen as strong, fully operational and untainted by any whiff of defeat or surrender. The campaign should go out with a bang and not a whimper. So, those who had supported the ceasefire initiative in order to try to bring an end to the horror they had experienced, and those who had regarded it as a sell-out, now found themselves involved in a massive stepping-up of the campaign of bombing and killing to make the job of ending the bombing and killing somewhat easier...

I remember well the evening in November, 1974, I think, that news came of a terrible bombing in Birmingham, England. Twenty-one civilians were killed and scores of others were maimed and injured when bombs exploded in pubs, seemingly without any warning. This occurred after an IRA man had been killed in nearby Coventry while trying to plant a bomb at a telephone exchange. I was in the company of one of the best-known Derry Republicans, and he was furious about the bombing. He stunned me by saying that if the IRA were found to be responsible for the bombing, he would have no hesitation in leaving the organization for good. I had never seen him so angry.

For my part, I was embarrassed at the thought of being associated with a deliberate anti-civilian bombing. I had to think seriously for the very first time about whether I had the independent qualities which my friend had – I found that I had no sense of an existence independent of the IRA, primarily because I had given my life to it, was on the run from police and Army, was going nowhere except to the graveyard or to prison, and had no other way out except by a ceasefire and a related deal or amnesty. It was not a cheerful realization. I was nothing if not a loner when it came to operations, but the discovery that I had sold my soul to the organization was repellent to me, and made me thirst for a life apart from the IRA.

IRA G.H.Q. released a press statement denying any involvement in the Birmingham pub bombings, and the veracity of this was not questioned by anyone. We took it for granted that G.H.Q. would not lie. The fact that the IRA was responsible, and that G.H.Q. did lie, did not become public knowledge for some years, by which time I was already an ex-member.

In November, 1974, back at the ceasefire, mention of talks between Republicans and Protestant Churchmen was briefly made, but details were kept very secret. Brigades might be expected to get reports on the progress, but on this occasion they were few and far between. To quell any damaging rumors or defeatist talk, G.H.Q. persons began to make the rounds to offer miserly details about the negotiations. The mere fact of their doing so was indicative of the seriousness of the ceasefire initiative.

The Big Push began before it had even been signaled and, it seems to me now, quickly got out of hand. In the run up to the Christmas ceasefire of 1974, we lost too many volunteers killed, injured and captured in the haste to get too many bombs to targets. Some inexperienced and not fully trained young lads were asked to go out to plant bombs, and they died in the attempt to do so. Others were injured, captured and imprisoned. I was not told about some of the operations, or else I was not consulted about the person being given the task of dealing with the explosives' side of things.

On one occasion when a young lad I was in the process of training was killed by the premature explosion of a bomb he was attempting to plant, I was livid that I had not been asked about him so that I might say definitively that he was not yet qualified to do it. His superior officer in the explosives' field had left the city, and again, I had not been told. His brother, knowing none of this, attacked me almost physically when he saw me, thinking that I had been involved in the decision to send him out, when in fact I hadn't. I couldn't give him any of the details which would have shown him otherwise. I began to wonder if the prize justified the cost.

Worst of all, when I was out of Derry in December, and had closed down some of my flats which I had run as bomb factories, I was shocked to hear on the afternoon television news that there had been an explosion in a flat in Crawford Square and that a young girl had been critically injured and taken to hospital.

I was so stunned by the news that I almost vomited and could not get rid of the feeling of nausea for some hours. The flat was mine, but there wasn't supposed to be anything in it of an explosive nature. The girl, Ethel, worked with me as closely as a sister, and was undoubtedly the most dedicated volunteer I had ever met. I knew her boyfriend, and had always tried to minimize the risks she took with and for me, and they were many. I would have easily given my life to preserve hers. Now I learned that, when I had told her she was inoperative, she had somehow or other been reactivated in my absence, and had been injured in a premature explosion, and was critically ill. Ethel died a few days later.

A newspaper report stated that a man had been seen running away from the flat, but no-one in the IRA had done so. God knows if anyone did run away from the area. Possibly it was a civilian who didn't want to be there when the Army and police arrived. However, on my return to Derry, a number of people asked me if I had been the person who ran away. I was angered by the insulting question, and simply replied, "Do you think I would have left Ethel if I had been there?" I felt powerless to dispel the rumors, though more IRA people knew than didn't know that I hadn't even been in Derry. I was extremely sensitive to the possibility that Ethel's family might think I had left her injured. I was angry with the Big Push, which had now cost the lives of some people who had been so close to me. So many of the deaths in IRA ranks were, in my opinion, avoidable, but caution had been set aside. I thought that the imminent ceasefire, for which I had voiced support, had better work after this additional suffering.

Then at Christmas, the IRA leadership announced in a statement to the press that the ceasefire was a reality. The media made much of it, and churchmen and most politicians blessed the good sense which had brought it about. The ongoing talks between the British Government and the IRA were condoned, if not celebrated.

In the weeks that followed, details began to emerge of the progress being made in direct negotiations between the IRA and the British Government. First and foremost, the IRA was given maps showing Catholic ghetto areas marked in green, and the assurance was given that the Army would not arrest persons within these marked areas. That meant even persons on the most wanted list. Homes would not be raided either, from which it followed that wanted men could go home. The Protestant police force, the Royal Ulster Constabulary, it was said, was not involved in the ceasefire, but was prevented from effecting any arrests in the green areas by virtue of the fact that the British Army would not give it escorting cover.

The British Government set up Incident Centers staffed by civil servants from the Northern Ireland Office. They undertook to provide instant remedial action in response to complaints from the IRA about Army breaches of the ceasefire. Similarly, the Government could reach by telephone the IRA commanders and demand that they remedy breaches or potential problems stemming from the IRA side.

We had one critical meeting of Derry Brigade Staff officers in January, 1975, which, viewed retrospectively, resulted in a terrible irony. At the meeting, we were discussing the flaws which we could see in the arrangements. The single big one was still the fact that the heavily armed Protestant Royal Ulster Constabulary was not involved in the ceasefire arrangements, was not trusted by the British Government, and was not trusted by the IRA either, and might therefore be expected to try to breach the ceasefire at every opportunity. We assumed that they would inevitably view a deal between the IRA and the British Government as a sell-out of the Ulster Protestant position.

We were asked about, among other things, what the Derry Brigade's response should be to an RUC breach of the ceasefire. I argued hotly that the RUC should know in no uncertain terms that if it breached the ceasefire, if it felt that it could take advantage of the IRA because the IRA's hands were tied by ceasefire negotiations, it should learn a lesson to the contrary; allowing the RUC free reign would result in none of us being safe. Little did I know that, when Fate played its hand, I was going to be the very person at the centre of an RUC breach of the ceasefire...

I got some bad news which was that while every other volunteer in the Derry Brigade could go home without fear of being arrested, I could not, nor could a well-known Derry girl. My two ounces of gelignite in 10 Downing Street were indeed more heinous than merely killing Brits in Northern Ireland. I remained tied to safe billets, where I had a task explaining that while the ceasefire applied to everyone else, it did not yet apply to me. Many prominent Republicans and people with a military background did not fully trust the British, and feared a mass-arrest operation. These people still used safe houses, or billets, and I spent my time largely with a very prominent Derry Republican. We did not fully trust the ceasefire after we had made a rare trip to his home for a cup of tea and a chat with his mother in the heart of the Bogside. Fifteen minutes later, we left for security reasons. We walked the few steps to the end of the little street and around the corner. Right in front of us were three Army jeeps from which armed soldiers were leaping. Two officers were stunned to recognize us, we were stunned to see them, and they looked as excited as if they were about to kill two turkeys for Christmas... We ran like lightning back up the street, and into an alley and away to a nearby safe house. The soldiers followed but we lost them easily. We thought it was very possible that the soldiers had intended to take out two prominent people, call it an unintentional breach of the ceasefire and then apologize after the fact.

For all my distrust, I did want the ceasefire to work. To keep my explosives' officers at work of some sort, and to change the nature of the work in which they were engaged, I thought up a useful community service which they could do with me. There was a row of pensioners' houses near the top of Beechwood Avenue and it occurred to me that it would be a service to these old people who had suffered so much disruption to their lives during the previous seven years to install a bell and or a light above the front door, with many switches or pushes around their houses, which they might use to call for help if they were taken ill or fell while alone indoors. I spoke to Brigade about purchasing items necessary for the job, and even went to electrical contractors to price the supply. I was disgusted to learn later that someone from the Brigade Staff had mentioned it in talks with an individual from the unrelated Bogside Community Association, which immediately stole the idea and revamped it as, I think, the "Buy a Light, Save a Life" campaign. I had no objection to the B.C.A. campaign, I just thought it undermined my endeavor to turn my explosives' officers into something different. I also felt I could tell certain persons on the Brigade Staff nothing that would not be carried to other people! I cast around for something else for my EO's to do, without immediate success.

Then word came to me that I could go home. I did not immediately do so, because I did not trust the RUC. I did go one evening with an IRA friend to a pub in the city centre where I had worked as a teenager to earn extra pocket money, and let my face be seen again. Lots of people came over to shake hands and wish us well in the new peace. I introduced my friend to a girl in the bar who had grown up as a neighbor of mine, and they later married and had two children...

I was asked to be Best Man at my eldest brother's wedding in Donegal in April 1975 and I did so and had a nice time. I had gone out with one or two girls and it hadn't been a bad experience at all. With all this rich diet of normality, I came to think that I had been a bit silly and extreme in my failure to put my trust in a ceasefire to which I had given my support. I began to think about home, and about how I would have to adapt for work and for the future. I thought about my studies and university. I decided to go home for a bit.

My mother had sold our large Clarendon Street house after my father had died, because only she, my kid brother and one of my sisters were at home. She had purchased a beautiful modern bungalow in Castleview Park in the outskirts of Derry beside the Catholic ghetto of Shantallow. The bungalow had a garden at the front and a lawn at the rear. I looked forward to a bit of gardening.

After a number of short, careful visits, I went home a full five months into the ceasefire, on Thursday, May 8th, 1975, and went to a nursery to buy a cherry-blossom tree, which I then planted in the front garden. It was a beautifully sunny day, with a mild breeze. I stripped to the waist and began to mow the grass of the back lawn barefoot. My mother called me into the kitchen after midday to eat some lunch, and I went in and sat at the table. As I picked up a knife and fork, I noticed two well-dressed young men approaching the back door of the kitchen. It opened to reveal them pointing pistols at my head, and shouting, "You are under arrest! Do not move! Raise your hands above your head!"

I was at something of a disadvantage, being unarmed, naked to the waist and barefoot, sitting down, under the impression that the public ceasefire meant that the conflict was over, but I was obviously mistaken. I said, "Okay!" and got up slowly. I saw my mother putting her hands to her face. The plainclothes cops grabbed my arms and dragged me out of the kitchen, around the rear of the house towards the front, where a large car was parked. Two more plainclothes stood gazing around the small, neat estate for opposition which was never going to come, given that everyone else was on ceasefire. They put me in the back seat of the car, and roared off towards Victoria Barracks. I noticed an Army foot patrol at the end of the street. So much for ceasefire agreements with the British, I thought to myself. The car journey passed in silence.

On arrival at Victoria Barracks, which must have been a lonely, un-characteristically quiet place for the previous five months of the ceasefire, there was not much activity. I was taken directly to a room where I was sat in a chair, and kept under guard by my armed shadows. What I was likely to do, unarmed and almost naked as I was, and under orders from the IRA to be inactive? A smallish, balding older man came over to me, bent down and, with his head on its side, said a number of times into my face, "Shane Paul O'Doherty, can you hear me? You are under arrest – can you hear me? You are under arrest. You will be questioned and charged – can you hear me?" Does he think I'm deaf? Does he really expect me to hold a conversation with him? I was intent on keeping silent, in line with IRA practice. I ignored him.

They put me in a cell in the basement, locked me in and left me. I looked at the walls. They were covered with the names of IRA men who had been held there over the years. I did not add mine, but only because I had no pen. I wandered slowly around the cell thinking that peace after all was but a dream, and was not going to become a reality. Too many people wanted to keep the strife going, and were not content to see a negotiated end, believing that a victory of one side over the other was possible. I knew it was not.

I was now out of the game, more or less. I was going to be a remote observer of the game outside in the world, while I tuned in to the inside world of prison. Of course, the Derry Brigade of the IRA was going to feel extremely betrayed by the British Government's attitude to the ceasefire, if the Incident Centers did not order my release or somehow or other secure it. There was no way that the IRA could allow individual volunteers to be arrested at will by the Royal Ulster Constabulary, or this would be regarded as a fine game by the Brits, who could hold the IRA to a ceasefire, while using the RUC to break it and pick off specific people. There was obviously going to be some major reaction.

After a while, I was taken upstairs by uniformed constables and pushed into a small, narrow room where two detectives were waiting for me. I was still barefoot and naked to the waist. It was not possible to still the beating heart, as I faced up to my first interrogation, having heard so many graphic details of the brutal, sadistic treatment practiced on friends arrested previously. However, there was a counterbalancing state of mind, a strange relaxation stemming from the end of it all, the end of tension, fear, effort, superconsciousness, anticipation of death, injury, arrest – it was all over, all behind me, and I was alive! What could two buffoons in suits do to me that would even remotely add up to what I had been doing to myself, to what the situation had done to us all? I was getting into a relaxation that I had never before experienced. It was beginning to dawn on me that I was out of the game.

I was sat in a chair against a wooden table which was in the form of a box – there was undoubtedly a microphone in it, leading to a tape-recorder elsewhere. Of the detectives, one was cleanshaven and undoubtedly as fanatical in his view that Ulster should remain Protestant and British for ever as I was in mine that the British should get out of Ireland and that Ireland should be united; the other was small and fat, with a Mexican-style black moustache. I was insulted by their trying the hard man/soft man approach. Did I look that naive? The Moustache attempted to become hysterically threatening and violent, while Cleanshaven pretended to have to pin him against the wall to defend me from a violent attack. He meanwhile made soothing offers to me, such as if I played ball with him, he would see that I was not harmed, etc.

I had my eyes fixed on a point not on the wall, held myself in a near-trance, and ignored the not-very-successful thespians. They seemed as embarrassed by their routine as comedians who were failing to raise a smile. They came close and slowed things down, to allow for tension and threat to be rebuilt again. They stood behind and beside me, referring to various attacks against Army and police in which I had been involved. One slapped the back of my head slowly but firmly while the other told me that there were various angry police officers waiting outside for a chance get at me. I did not react.

They called me names, and offered to fight me one at a time, man to man they said, if a coward like me could even be described as a man. I breathed audibly down my nose to express my boredom. They pushed my shoulders and offered, "Come on you coward! Now's your chance for face-to-face combat!" I was thinking to myself in my trance-world, "I have been shot at by the Army and escaped. I have been blown up by explosives and survived. Relax. The hard part is over."

The detectives decided to try to press other buttons. They named friends of mine whom they had maltreated when things had been bad, and described in detail what they had done to them. They promised that before many more hours were passed, they would have practiced all of it on me. They were giving me this time for anticipation of it, they said.

It got to the stage where I wanted to say to them, "Hit me, you mouthing bastards! Hit me! Try to break me with your fists, 'cause you'll be disappointed!" But later I wanted to say, "Get it over with! I'm tired of waiting!" I began to understand why some people ended up prepared to sign statements pleading guilty to the murders of everybody from Jesus Christ to John F. Kennedy. It occurred to me that I could bring it all to a head by attacking them first...

Then I was pulled up from the chair, and pushed to the door of the room where a gaggle of black uniformed RUC men were waiting to take me downstairs to the cell again. This time, they herded me along a different route, curiously walking behind me. As I was directed to go through a particular room, I noticed that there were two sterling sub-machine guns, with magazines inserted in them, lying on a table past which I had to walk.

In that moment, I was being offered the wildest temptation that a tired, pressurized, stressed youth could imagine, a loaded weapon with which to change the whole situation! A glance behind showed me that my shadows were holding their weapons pointed at me, stupidly hoping that I would make a go for a machine gun that was inevitably unloaded.

I was barely in the cell, still naked to the waist and barefoot, when I was taken upstairs again. Cleanshaven was smiling. He told me they were bugging the phones of the incident centers, that my arrest had stirred up a hornets' nest, but that I was definitely not going to be released. He relaxed momentarily and became conversational, telling me that they had a whole room devoted to me and to the intelligence and evidence they had gathered on me.

Next Cleanshaven got ready to really throw me – I could hear it in his voice. He asked me what I thought they had found in my Clarendon Street home. I did not reply. He held up a half-sheet of paper on which was a child's neat cursive script. I was so embarrassed that I blushed inside and out when I read my own handwriting: "I, Shane Paul O'Doherty, want to fight and, if necessary, die for Ireland's freedom. Signed: *Shane Paul O'Doherty*." It was dated about 1965, when I was ten years old. Despite the decade that had passed, I distinctly remembered the evening when I wrote that patriotic note to posterity and hid it under the floorboard in the attic.

Cleanshaven told me that the police had been emptying my family's refuse-bin outside my home for years to examine the contents for signs of my presence. He said they had expected a huge, detonator-chewing desperado, but were disappointed to capture someone skinny, intense and silent. I was pushed into the chair again, with the promise that I was going to be broken before the evening was out. Cleanshaven then began to name friends of mine who had been shot dead, or killed by their own bombs. He described some of their injuries. He went out of the room, saying that he had a treat for me.

He returned with a thick folder and began to lay out on the table in front of me large, black and white photographs of the naked, bloodied, injured, stitched body of Ethel Lynch. The photographs had been taken in the hospital morgue, and Ethel's eyes had been opened and her naked body variously arranged for these shots. I couldn't believe that they had taken these photographs and kept them specially for me, for the day that they hoped to interrogate me. Perhaps they were in the habit of keeping such pictures for private Armed Forces' circulation. I was almost vomiting with the horror of the photos. Cleanshaven was shouting that I had murdered her, that I had run away from the flat after the explosion, that I had betrayed her by cowardice, that they were going to charge me with her murder, that her family would think that I had run out on her, and everyone else in Derry would think likewise! "Look at her body! Look at her injuries! Look at her blood! Look at her stitches! You murdered her! You are a coward! Coward!"

I began to get angry, angrier than I had felt in a long time. I was staring at the large photographs of Ethel's open, yet dead eyes, and nothing they might have tried, no pain, no threat, could have equaled or overcome my anger. I was inviolable from that point on. They called off that interrogation some time later.

Uniformed cops took me to the basement cell once more, still offering insults and threats. I couldn't have cared less. The next interrogation was a formality – Cleanshaven read out a list of incidents in which they believed I had been involved, and asked me if I wished to say anything about each. I replied every time, "Nothing to say." This made me recall the contents of a note which an arrested bomber had sent out of prison in order to tell what he had been asked during his interrogation and what he had said. The gist of it was that he put a lot of his jobs down to me, because he didn't think I would ever be arrested, owing to his belief that I would never again put myself within range of arrest by the British after the London bombings. I suspected that a good many of the jobs put to me were his.

I was formally charged with two Derry letter bombs after that, and told that I would definitely be going to court the next day, which was Saturday. My sister was allowed in to see me briefly and brought some clothes and shoes so that I might be clothed at last. With the formal charging, and the arrangement of a definite court appearance, the interrogations were over. Cleanshaven and Moustache returned for a conversation, "off the record" they said, which meant nothing whatsoever. One asked me why I had never bombed the houses of police officers. I replied that while the British Army and Royal Ulster Constabulary had practiced a policy of terrorizing wives and children of Republicans by constantly raiding homes and wrecking them, the IRA in Derry felt that attacks on the enemy's families, wives and children, were not desirable. Cleanshaven showed his true colors, and did more than hint at police collusion with Protestant Loyalist paramilitaries: "Well, Shane, if you had organized or taken part in attacks against our families, we would have spoken to the lads up the country [loyalist paramilitaries] about relatives of yours." This was a clear threat aimed at totally innocent relations of mine who were very vulnerable.

Saturday came, and I was told that I was not going to appear in a special court in Catholic Derry, but in Protestant Coleraine some thirty miles away for security reasons. I was handed over to four young detectives, handcuffed to two of them and put into a large, fast car for the journey. As we drove out of Victoria Barracks, we fitted in between two Army jeeps, but once out of the city, our driver accelerated away and drove to Coleraine without them, making insulting remarks about the Army. They were more insulting about the Army than about me. On arrival at Coleraine, where the police station and court were combined in one building, the detectives got involved in a bitter row with the uniforms about who should fingerprint me, and the uniforms had to do it. I appeared in court a short time later for a matter of seconds and was remanded in custody to Belfast prison. The breach of the ceasefire was now irreparable, and there would definitely be retaliation, as the RUC well knew.

I was driven off to Belfast by my four detectives, who once more ditched their Army escort. They managed to get lost in the Republican area of the Ardoyne in Belfast before finding their way to the prison. There was panic in the car when we got into a cul de sac in Ardoyne, surrounded by IRA murals and propaganda. The driver was shouted at by the others until he got back onto the Crumlin Road near the prison.

My first experience of Belfast prison was unforgettable not for the penal side of things, but for an atmosphere of the most extreme religious sectarianism and hatred I had ever known then or since. I was entering the prison on May 10th, 1975, when the Protestant paramilitaries were killing Roman Catholics as their form of protest at the British Government's ceasefire with the IRA, and in order to draw the IRA in Belfast into a sectarian conflict. Virtually every prison warder was a Protestant with an aggressively political outlook. To a man they hated Republicans, IRA people, and – since they saw no distinction – Roman Catholics. They let new arrivals to the prison know this immediately.

Because it was the weekend, instead of being taken directly to "A" wing, the IRA wing of the prison, (which the IRA prisoners themselves controlled and ran), as would happen on a weekday, I was to be placed on a non-political wing, "B" wing, in solitary confinement until the Monday. This meant that I was not behind the defensive shield of the IRA-run wing and was fair game for the bitter warders, who had access to my file and knew exactly who I was and what the police suspected me of having done on the outside.

When my name was called out, Shane Paul O'Doherty, its Irishness alone indicated that I was a "Taig", a pejorative term for a Roman Catholic, a Nationalist who must believe that Britain should get out of Ireland, that Ireland should be united, that the Protestant State of Northern Ireland had had its day. Worse, I was an IRA volunteer, someone who actually warred against the State, and who had been caught and now must be made to pay.

The warders didn't even let their eyes meet mine, used frozen speech to instruct me as to what I should or should not do, spoke to each other as if I were not there: "Cecil, here's another Taig bastard for B wing. A murdering IRA bastard. These fuckers should be taken out and shot. Prison's too good for them. Take the bastard away." I was escorted to B wing, and walked to a line of about ten or twelve cells which were cut off from the rest of the wing by a wire cage. This was a small extra punishment unit for overflow from the basement one, or a holding unit for prisoners received at the weekend. Each cell was furnished with a metal bed cemented into the floor, a chair, and a fixed table against the wall. I was told that I might not even sit on the bed until after seven-thirty p.m. and locked in. I sat on the chair for a while, broke the rules and stood on the bed frame to see a little out of the high, tiny barred windows – I could see nothing but the drab, miserable, crumbling brickwork of the old prison. A disgusting mess was served on a metal tray with brown liquid that went by the name of tea. I could taste neither. Eventually I made up the bed from the folded, stinking blankets and threadbare sheets, got in and dozed off for the first time since the Thursday morning...

Later I heard the clanking of chains and keys and the sound of a metal door being slowly and ponderously opened, with bolts being drawn back – I thought I was dreaming. My cell door was being opened in the dead of night. Even I knew that this was against every prison rule of security, since cell keys are never on a wing by night. I sat up nervously. A very tall, very heavy warder came in the door, silhouetted against the light outside. He asked, "Are you that fucking bastard from Londonderry arrested the other day?" Still disoriented and unsure of where I was and what was happening, I mumbled "Yes."

"Your fucking comrades shot dead a young constable of the RUC this afternoon. Shot him in the back, the cowardly bastards, in retaliation for your arrest. He's dead. I just wanted you to know that his father is the Principal Warder in charge of this wing, and we're going to fucking kill you tomorrow. Think on that tonight." With that he slammed the door, shot the bolts and marched away. I began to realize that the ceasefire had only ended one phase of violence.

I knew that the next day, and the days after it, were not going to be very kind to me. I could not sleep, dressed at dawn and waited for the morning attack, which the warder had promised. I thought it was ironical that these Protestant warders, many of them extreme evangelicals, were going to begin their Sunday morning by beating the hell out of me. Sunday, I mused, was supposed to be a day of rest.

Keys jangled outside and a lot of footsteps came to my cell door. At the word, "Ready," the door was thrown open, and a crowd of prison warders charged at me, fists flailing and boots kicking. The space between the iron bed and the table attached to the wall was so narrow, that they could not all get to me at once, but then they quickly grabbed my hair and pulled me out to where they could punch and kick me better, calling me a "fucking Fenian bastard", a "fucking IRA cunt", a "fucking Taig bastard". I felt an extreme hatred of these warders. They left me on the floor, barely aware of where I was, barely able to feel any pain or taste any blood. There was nothing I could do but put up with this maltreatment.

I had learned one lesson already: that we in Derry, who lived all our lives in a city which was majority Catholic and Nationalist, were living in a dream world. The war that we were able to wage against the British Army alone was not addressing the real problem – the million Protestants who were definitely there, who were a very real majority in Northern Ireland, and who wanted to remain free of a United Ireland. They were prepared to use their position of being the State, with their police force and the locally-raised Ulster Defense Regiment, with the control of the prisons where they virtually held Catholic and Republican people as hostages, to fight a war all on their own, separate from the British Army. It had been clear to me as soon as the Protestant detectives had scorned their British Army escort of jeeps and boasted of their independence in arresting me and as soon as I entered a Protestant prison as an enemy Catholic and was liable to be killed. I got a few more beatings that Sunday, and lay on the floor to try to shield as much of my body as was able to touch it.

On Monday morning, the regular warders, most of whom had had the weekend off, came on duty and wanted to pay their respects to me in similar fashion. I was against the wall, instinctively using the narrow space between the bed and the table as a defense, when the door opened. Through eyes that could barely open and see, I watched, again in my slow motion, new warders' faces running towards me. Oddly, one of them held a newspaper. I hardly felt the punches or the kicks, or being grabbed by the hair again and dragged into a more accessible part of the cell. One warder, who led the attacks from then on, pulled my hair in such a way that my face and the newspaper were inches apart. He shouted, "Look, you

Fenian bastard! Look! What do you say to that? Your fucking bishop agrees with us!"

I could see the Catholic daily newspaper, "The Irish News", and a large headline which covered the shooting of the police constable and the Lord Bishop's comments on same, but nothing about the breach of the ceasefire.

The weekday warders planned to do more than beat me up. Their leader, whose name I still recall, ripped the bed sheets into long strips and took them over to the high window-bars saying, "Listen, you bastard, this is your only way out! Either you do it, or we'll make your life a living hell! And if you don't do it, we will!" With that they left the cell, but put a young trainee warder outside my cell door to constantly switch on and off the light all day. Even when he tired of his mind-bending task, I heard them yell at him to keep it going...

At about nine a.m. they came back in and grabbed me, dragged me out of the cell and up the wing, while other prisoners watched from various landings. I was taken into an office, where a prison Governor sat behind a desk. I realized that this was an internal court to hear charges against me of offences against the disciplinary code. My offences were nonexistent, but the Governor nonetheless found me guilty and sentenced me to three days solitary confinement. This meant that, instead of transferring me to the IRA wing on Monday morning, they were ensuring that I would be kept behind the wire on "B" wing where they could get at me whenever they wanted.

The prison Governor never once looked up from the paperwork in front of him to view my injuries, to see that no prison warders were injured, to see clearly my condition, which was one by now of total exhaustion and stress. I was learning my lesson early that prisons and prison warders are outside the law and can torture prisoners without fear of punishment. I have to admit that when, some years later, this prison Governor was shot dead in an IRA ambush, I was so bitter toward him that I could not find in my heart any sympathy whatsoever.

The irony of it all was compounded by the arrival outside the prison a day or so later, while I still languished behind the wire on B wing, of the

RUC band to play the dead march as the funeral left the Principal Warder's house nearby. The band was clearly audible throughout the prison. The warders on B wing came in for another go at me to the musical accompaniment, though, without any sleep, rest, wash or food, I was hardly worth punching or kicking any more. Shortly after the funeral, Principal Warder Clarke, the only Catholic I ever came across in Belfast prison, came to my cell. He took careful note of my injuries and condition, and told me he was having me moved to the IRA wing whatever the warders on B wing said. The B wing warders were congregating behind him, calling us both names. He ignored it all, and took me to A wing. The IRA prisoners told me that they'd informed the prison Governor that there would be a riot if I was not brought to their wing forthwith.

The B wing warders were not going to be put off by the fact that I had been removed from their control. As I was coming back from a legal visit, I was told I also had a social visit. I asked to deposit my legal papers in my cell first, because I had asked my lawyer to record the names of the prison warders who had threatened my life, and their names were on my papers. The warders said there was no need, I might deposit the papers in the search-room by the visiting room and no-one would look at them. I went to be searched and found the leader of the gang on B wing waiting for me. He picked up the papers, saw his name on them, rang the alarm bell and accused me of trying to take his name out to my visitors for communication to the IRA. It was an absurd accusation, since I had asked to deposit my papers back on A wing, and since I had merely to speak his name to my visitors, or smuggle it out. However, it was sufficient to get me back into solitary behind the wire on B wing, where the maltreatment began again, while every authority in the prison turned away its eyes. I was growing extremely bitter against the prison system.

I was appointed to an IRA position on A wing, which meant debriefing those men newly imprisoned on what they had said during interrogation, or on what had been said to them by police. I would write this down and smuggle it out to the IRA unit from which they had come, so that their units could engage in damage limitation, if necessary. Within weeks, I had fallen foul of Belfast Brigade of the IRA over the question of recognition of British courts, which I opposed, and which they sometimes permitted. It led to anomalies in the prison, where some Belfast people could recognize the courts which were going to try them, while persons from other areas of Northern Ireland could not. I was dismissed from my post just for raising the question, but bigger issues concerned me by then.

Firstly, whereas I had imagined that I was the only arrested volunteer during the ceasefire, I found that men were being arrested on a daily basis in Belfast, where a virtual sectarian war raged on the streets. Catholic pubs were being bombed without warning by Protestant paramilitaries, and IRA units retaliated by targeting Protestant pubs frequented by Protestant paramilitaries. Protestant paramilitaries shot Catholics dead on a regular basis, and local IRA units, coming under pressure from the local community, shot Protestants dead in retaliation. In Derry, we didn't believe this happened, thinking that the targeted Protestants were paramilitaries, but I was learning that many targets were Protestants pure and simple. I met the volunteers who shot them.

It soon became clear that the ceasefire barely applied in Belfast. Operations against the British Army had been suspended, but war against the Protestant paramilitaries went on. A ceasefire which did not include the Protestant paramilitaries, the wholly Protestant police force and Ulster Defense Regiment was hollow indeed. How long could it last?

I spent the summer of 1975 in Belfast prison, mostly in the prison yard in what sunshine hit Belfast, where we could hear the booms of the explosions that destroyed Catholic and then Protestant pubs, and the shots that pierced Catholic and then Protestant flesh. It was a bad summer in Northern Ireland. In September, I got good news and bad news. The good news was that when I went to court for a regular weekly remand, the charges against me were dropped and I was released. The bad news was that London Metropolitan police were waiting outside the courtroom to re-arrest me, charge me with London letter bombings, and fly me to London aboard a Royal Air Force ministerial jet.

The press described the arrest of a wanted London bomber, a

"mastermind", an active IRA man who had just been captured by brilliant detective work and brought immediately to London for his just deserts... No-one there knew, or cared, that the British Government had been in a ceasefire with the IRA, that there had been substantial negotiations between the parties, that I had been inactive for nearly six months when arrested contrary to the ceasefire terms, and that I'd spent four more months in Belfast prison.

My poor mother! She had taken more than a little comfort from the fact that I had been arrested and taken out of the struggle where I might lose my life at any time. She thought that imprisonment at least guaranteed my security and imposed a sort of unchanging order upon my existence. I had told her nothing of the reality of life in Belfast prison. Now she had to take in my surprise release, re-arrest by London police and launch into the national news headlines for London bombings. I was still putting her through hell!

It was not just the leaves which fell in the autumn of 1975, but the longest ceasefire since the troubles began, as became clear with the resumption of London bombings and the new phenomenon of shootings there, when Ross McWhirter, who had offered a reward for information contributing to the arrest of the IRA cell operating in London, was shot dead at his front door by the IRA.

I spent a whole year on remand in Brixton prison, London, before my trial at the Old Bailey in September 1976. I was a Category "A" Top Security prisoner, which meant that I had a single cell in either of two security units, and a lot of time to think. Now that I was out of the game, I allowed myself the luxury and the freedom of reading whatever I wanted. I was interested in morality, and, in particular, in the doctrine of the just war. Since I already knew how to make a war, I wanted to learn how to make a peace, a just peace, and how to maintain it. Everything I read I studied with a view to justifying the violence I had practiced.

Two Jesuit priests were sharing the chaplaincy of Brixton prison, Frs. Anthony Lawn and James Langan. The latter was a part-time stand-in for the full-time Prison Service Chaplain, Fr. Lawn. Fr. Lawn was not at all popular with the Irish prisoners, since he was a former British Army officer turned Jesuit, an avowed English Nationalist. He told the story of how he had demanded that his passport describe him as "English" instead of, as in the more usual format, "British". He did give me straight answers to straight questions, and, after a long period of disliking him, I came to respect his quirky, honest, idiosyncratic nature. Years later, when he got a central part alongside Jeremy Irons in the film "The Mission", playing a Jesuit missionary to Latin America, I thought he did not need to act the Jesuit zealot.

Fr. Langan, however, was instantly lovable. He had a weak heart and had to sit down to say Mass, which meant that, since I was in top security conditions and alone, he and I could have Mass at a small table, in the form of a meal. He had been very close to the then quite famous Price sisters, members of an IRA bomb team who had been on a very long hunger-strike in Brixton prison protesting for a transfer back to a Northern Ireland. Their campaign, during which they were force-fed, mobilized a lot of opinion in their support. They had just been transferred to Northern Ireland, I was told, as part of the ceasefire deal, before it broke down completely. Fr. Langan had loved the Price sisters. He told me that he respected them so much that he had never been able to say to them that one of their bombs, which exploded outside the Old Bailey Central Criminal Court, had injured his sister who was a barrister. The Price sisters had obviously made a considerable impact on Brixton prison, because the Education Officer spent hours telling me about his respect for them. The Prison Governor told me that their hunger-strike had damaged his health and nerves. He died soon after.

Fr. Lawn had an adversarial quality to his communication that I found quite stimulating. I asked him once where I should look for proof that his Catholic God definitely existed. He replied, simply, "In the Gospels, of course." I read the Gospels for the first time ever in one sitting. I was extraordinarily taken by how the personality of the man, Jesus Christ, came across from the four accounts, by his radical views and activities, opposition to hypocrisy, dedication to the poor, and by his constant revolutionary references to the love of enemies. There was an idealism in his message that immediately appealed to me, that was pure and undefiled by compromises or mistakes.

I was beginning to feel the problem of the cracks in my Republican idealism stemming from the armed struggle and its many victims, but I realized that it was a bad time to get religion, so I put it off for a while, at least until after my trial. I definitely wanted to go through my trial as an IRA man, scorning British concepts of justice for Ireland and for Irishmen who fought against the British occupation of Ireland.

But the biggest blow to my beliefs and to my idealism was yet to come. It was part of the legal process that a charged person should receive a copy of all of the evidence intended for use in the trial. I got this huge sheaf of statements, called depositions, in November 1975 and sat down to read them one night in my solitary cell in Brixton prison. They told the stories of each and every letter bomb and of the persons injured by them, and included the reports of medical people on the injuries sustained. These people were innocent civilians whose names had not been on the bombs and I was horrified. Here in black and white, was the plainest proof that my use of violence had transformed me from an idealist on high moral ground to an offender with a seemingly endless list of human rights' violations to his name. None of this reeked of justice. I was coming face to face finally with the consequences of my long-distance bombings and I was not happy. There was no justification whatsoever for these injuries, and I was deeply sorry for the selfish and callous disregard I had shown for civilian casualties at a time when I had been cock-a-hoop about my bombing successes.

I was still trying to believe that it was justified to injure or kill members of the British Armed Services, or of their political wing, government ministers who supported or condoned the British military occupation of a part of Ireland.

I was trying to answer a hundred questions all at once: Did God exist, and what was He/She/They like? Did a judgmental crematorium wait to roast those who did not obey the Roman Catholic church? Was there a perspective on God and afterlife which countered the *dies illae, dies irae* wrath and judgment-oriented Catholic view? Was a war only just if you won it? Why didn't the British agonize about their violence in other people's countries? In the midst of my deliberations, I was interrupted.

CHAPTER 7

Near to Treason

I was taken to my political trial at the Old Bailey on 5th September, 1976, before Lord Justice Thesiger, great-grandson, they told me, of the Irish patriot Lord Edward Fitzgerald. Sticking firmly to my principles, shaken though they had been, I refused to recognize the court, refused to plead, refused to take part, offered no mitigation, and spoke an indignant, contemptuous speech from the dock to which the geriatric Thesiger replied:

"That comes near to treason – you might still be open to a charge of treason!"

He was either so old or so bored by events that he nodded off constantly during the trial. In my speech from the dock, I had uttered an apology to "those innocent working-class persons accidentally and unintentionally injured by my bombs". This was, to my knowledge, the first time that an IRA volunteer had apologized publicly for injuries caused to innocent civilians. I had sent word to the Republican Movement that I was going to apologize publicly, and no-one had objected.

I had indicated to the court that I was not going to participate and that I did not require a 'full' trial, i.e. that I did not require the calling of every single witness. I did this primarily to save my victims the trauma of having to come before an Old Bailey court. As a result, the trial began on Monday morning and ended the following Friday afternoon. The police had repeatedly offered me a deal since my arrival in London. They explained to me that, if I were co-operative with them and supplied information about the organizational side of the London bombings, they would ensure I got a ten-year sentence, with the certainty of release on parole after one third of that period, i.e. three years and four months. Minus the time I had already spent in prison unconvicted, they were saying I could get out in two years. They named another prisoner I knew (who was not facing particularly serious charges) and told me that he had already accepted the deal. (The other prisoner later received the sentence and parole release which they had indicated.) They also explained that non-cooperation would bring about the opposite result. I already knew that the 'independence of the judiciary' meant that the police had the authority to determine a sentence in advance of the trial.

There was something distasteful about making a deal which would sell out friends and former comrades for a reduction in sentence. I was annoyed in anticipation of the hypocrites who would wring hands over the moral question of how long I should spend in prison when the police and judiciary regarded that as mere bargaining in pursuit of information. Would the hand-wringers confront the police and judiciary on the subject? I rejected the police offer of a deal out of hand, and every time they repeated it. I knew the consequences of such rejection.

Thesiger sentenced me to life imprisonment on each of the first thirty counts, and to twenty years concurrently on the thirty-first charge. I regarded his judgment as empty and morally meaningless. Holding to my decision not to recognizing the court, I did not appeal against the sentence.

The press didn't know quite how to handle the trial. Here, if the evidence was to be believed, was the mastermind of the London bombing campaign in the summer of 1973. He was eighteen years old then and a student. He was calm, intelligent, from a good family and yet driven to explode bombs in London. He sat in the dock of the court in a shirt, tie and jacket and looked respectable. None of the issues which had motivated him or his comrades had been addressed or analyzed. Even the serious papers turned to tabloid phraseology to deal with the unwelcome phenomenon: The Bomber Who Got Too Cocky... The Mastermind Who Got Caught... Thirty Life Sentences For IRA Terrorist...

Following my conviction, I was taken to Her Majesty's Prison, Wormwood Scrubs, in West London. A prison warder asked my name, date and place of birth. I replied, "Derry, Northern Ireland." "When did you first enter the United Kingdom?" he demanded. I replied that I had been born in Northern Ireland, but the warder persisted, "Yes, Paddy, but when did you first enter the United Kingdom?" I gave up and told him on the day I was born, which satisfied him. The fact that hundreds of British soldiers had died in Britain's attempt to prove that Northern Ireland was part of the United Kingdom had not impinged upon this British citizen at all.

After a time in a bare cell in the Reception area of the grimly-named prison, I was taken out to undress my civilian clothes. I took them off, and then refused to wear the prison uniform. The warders were taken aback and asked me why. I told them that I had been on a political wing of Belfast prison, and in line for political status after conviction for any IRA acts in Northern Ireland. I still regarded conviction for IRA explosives offences in London as political – this was after all, the United Kingdom – a political offence in one part must be a political offence in another. I had no intention of wearing criminal uniform. The warders phoned a higher authority after which I was told that I was being taken to "A" Wing Segregation Unit, the solitary confinement block. I was handed my blankets, sheets and pillow-case and, wearing one of the blankets across my shoulders, I walked barefoot through heavy rain and huge puddles to A Seg., with a security escort and Alsatian dog.

As I entered the solitary block, I met the R.C. prison chaplain, Fr. Gerry Ennis. His first and entirely partisan line to me was, "Put your clothes on!" The following day I told him that I wanted nothing to do with him, and I did not allow him to enter my cell for many months. Much later, he helped to gain permission for my mother to visit me (I was not allowed visits because I would not wear prison uniform), after which we talked and proceeded to become the closest of friends.

And so I entered a period of naked solitary confinement that was to last from September 10th 1976 until November 19th 1977. Initially, some of the warders tried to maltreat me in the solitary block, but Senior Officer Tanner who was in charge made it clear that there was going to be no messing with me while I was there, and made one warder apologize for harassing me. Tanner was a former Army officer who believed that rules applied to guards as much as to prisoners, and I grew to respect his evenhandedness and to like him a lot. I had a stubborn will and would have died before bowing the knee, but Tanner made sure that his fair treatment gave me no grounds for complaint; in return, he expected me not to hassle the staff of the solitary unit. He was one of a very few principled prison officers I met during my fourteen years in Her Majesty's prisons and I talked seriously with him about my situation.

Wearing nothing but a small towel around my waist for the sake of modesty, I felt the cold during the day when I was up and around. I made it a rule never to use the bed by day. After a few weeks, I no longer noticed the temperature, even on the coldest days, but, skinny as I was, I lost a tremendous amount of bodyweight just burning calories to keep warm. On my first morning in solitary, the prison medical service's view of me was expressed by one doctor at my cell door: "There are three types of prisoner, O'Doherty – the mad, the sad and the bad. You are all three." Obviously a reader of the tabloid press. This particular doctor hated me on sight, and the prison warders often joked with me about the degree of that hatred, which even they found incredible.

I had two books with me initially: B.K.S. Iyengar's encyclopedic "Light On Yoga" and the Bible. I was able to purchase books by post, as long as I did not have more than six in my cell, and rotated them. I needed the yoga to keep me fit in the small cell, and to help me defeat tension, the main daily ingredient of prison life. I was reading the Bible from cover to cover for spiritual and mental exercise, and for evidence to justify my violence. I also purchased a copy of Norman Marrow's Quaker translation of the four gospels, which became my favorite. I bought books by post from the International Fellowship of Reconciliation, which published pamphlets on pacifism, justice issues, and non-violent revolution, all of which I desperately sought to understand. I joined the academically-oriented Howard League for Penal Reform, which regularly published articles about penology, criminology and ideas on victims' support schemes. I studied the life of one of my favorite political characters, Keir Hardie, who was associated with the founding of the Independent Labor Party in Britain.

My period in solitary confinement was one of intense consciousness for me, heightened by an accumulation of factors since I had expressed my support for the ceasefire some two years before. I did not ever want to let go of the fact that I had tried to make peace in my past, nor of the memory of what normality had been like during the ceasefire and before my arrest. My experiences of Belfast prison weighed heavily on me, in particular the sectarian nature of much of the conflict in that city which had come as a total surprise to me, and which put a huge question mark against the armed struggle overall. I had discussed the problem with some of the more prominent prisoners there, including Brendan "Bik" McFarlane, fated later to bear the burden of overall command of the IRA prisoners in the infamous "H" Blocks during the hungerstrikes.

Whatever my sympathy for IRA people who felt obligated to retaliate in kind for loyalist paramilitary murders of Catholics, I could not countenance sectarian murders, the retaliatory murders of civilians who happened to be Protestant. There was no justification whatsoever for such attacks and I was bitter that Brigades other than Derry had engaged in them. Nor could I accept the IRA's bombings causing risks to civilians in London greater than those offered to civilians back home in Derry or Belfast. The growing list of civilian casualties in Britain certainly implied that British civilian lives counted for less than Irish Catholic lives back home.

I had no experience of short or long periods of solitary confinement, and I was learning the hard way that the lonely human being seeks to meet every need in the self, seeks to perfect the self, and becomes extremely self-critical. I wondered about my own life and identity and the direction that I would take, in the light of my studies. I had stuck to my Republican principles in not recognizing the British court, but I now felt that, since I was buried alive in the bowels of the British prison system for a period of thirty life sentences and twenty years, I was the "freest" person on earth. I had paid my dues to the IRA, and to the British, and now began to feel the need for a sense of freedom, to be myself, to think for myself and to express my own views, not those of others. I had a sense that it was inevitable that I would leave the IRA, if for no other reason than to once more have individuality and an existence wherein I could be myself, something I had not experienced for years.

From the day when I was arrested in front of my mother, I had also to take account of the toll of it all on my family, perhaps too late to repair much of it, but I hoped better late than never. While I had been on the run, I could afford to be totally focused on the dangers and problems affecting my own life, while virtually ignoring my family. The regular prison visits I had received from my mother and from some of my brothers brought home to me a sense of the importance of family relationships, which I had definitely lost. The support they had given to me, plus the assurance of more to come in the long years ahead, made me feel not only a sense of gratitude, but also a sense of shame that I had made so many decisions without as much as considering the consequences for them. I wondered how I might have felt if, as a quiet, uninvolved family member, I had suddenly been catapulted into the limelight, and into danger, by a brother who had declared war on the British Government, the British Army, police and Loyalist paramilitaries, not forgetting the intelligence services which colluded with the Loyalists.

I had a strong sense that the debt of gratitude I owed my family might include a decision to leave the organization with which I had had a long affair, to return, like the prodigal son, to my home. I also thought that my withdrawal of my previously volunteered services would hardly matter to the IRA, since I had faded into the prison system anyway.

In tandem with my intense my search for my own identity, I was conducting a correspondence campaign to back up my protest for repatriation to Northern Ireland, where I'd been arrested and where my family and I lived. A 1960s Criminal Justice Act had provided for the facility: "The Responsible Minister may, on the application of a person serving a sentence of imprisonment or detention in any part of the United Kingdom, make an order for his transfer to another part of the United Kingdom, there to serve the remainder of his sentence, and for his removal to an appropriate institution in that part of the United Kingdom. I was quoting this in letters to prominent individuals who were interested in penal issues and in the fate of Irish prisoners in English prisons. I eventually wrote to the very Bishop of Derry whose comments after my arrest, and after the retaliatory shooting of the police constable, were thrust in my face by the warders who were assaulting me in Belfast prison. Bishop Edward Daly became like a father to me and stood by me for years while the British Home Office and prison system did their best to crush me.

Two M.P.s of the British Labor Party helped and influenced me greatly over the years. Andrew Bennett and Phillip Whitehead, my regular prison visitors for almost a decade, were brave men who taught me a lot about the worth of individual character. Their decision to visit and help was made at a time when the British tabloid press was calling for the hanging of IRA prisoners, and when MPs risked virulent campaigns of vilification for having contact with me. I learned that in any society there should be people willing and brave enough to reach out to enemies of that society. Apart from the indefatigable Derry M.P. and SDLP leader, John Hume, I looked across the Irish Sea to Ireland in vain for similarly brave elected representatives.

Lord Longford, the Catholic peer whose roots straddled the Irish Sea, and who had been visiting Irish Republican prisoners for some thirty-five years, also became a great friend and helper. He had known Eamonn De Valera and constantly debated Catholic and pacifist issues in his mind, and shared it all with me. Lord Hylton also later came to my aid, as did Cardinals Hume and O'Fiaich.

The police meanwhile made another attempt to offer me a new deal. Pretending that I was required for a visit from my lawyer, Gareth Pearce, the prison authorities walked me out of solitary confinement wearing nothing but a towel to the legal visiting room. They ushered me into the room and shut the door firmly behind me. As soon as I saw the two detectives, I demanded to be allowed to return to my cell, a demand which was not met until the police had made their offer. They said I'd spend twenty years in prison if I did not cooperate with them. I refused point blank.

Newspapers indicated that events outside had taken a marked turn for the worse. A reaction had set in against the fallen ceasefire, and violence had increased in severity. My prison protest was getting irregular coverage in Republican publications, usually alongside stories of IRA activity. On one occasion, an article adjoining one about me in "Republican News" told of a particularly horrific and fatal attack on a female soldier in Northern Ireland. It was a job which appalled me, and in which I would have had no part. I felt more keenly my guilt for the injuries I had accidentally caused to secretaries who had opened letter bombs addressed to their employers.

My embarrassment at being associated in print with that job transformed a vague, nebulous desire into a firm decision: I felt that I should express my views in the "Republican News", views which harked back to the late 1974 ceasefire period. I would question the use of the tactic of violence and the injustices and human rights' violations which our own counter-violence against the British had created. I thought that it was time to be identified for the views that I actually held now, rather than for the views that people expected or wished me to hold. I felt especially that my service to the IRA had earned me the right to express even unpopular views on the letters' page of the Republican newspaper. I wrote a letter which adequately expressed my views, and sent it out to a member of my family, asking that it be given to a prominent Derry Republican along with my request that it be printed in the letters' column of "Republican News".

Meanwhile, most of the people to whom I had written about my protest for transfer back to Northern Ireland responded that, by trying to force the British Home Office's hand, I would get nowhere. By refusing to conform to prison rules and clothing, they said, I was making it impossible for the System to accede to my request. The System could not be seen to give in to a protest for fear that it might be accused of fostering a hundred others. I was asked to give my parliamentary supporters a space in which to try their efforts, since I had the best possible case for transfer and fulfilled every criterion admitted by the British for repatriation. My family had also put this argument to me more than once. So, after fourteen months naked in solitary, in November 1977 I eventually decided to test this theory, to conform and to give up my protest. However, I reserved the right to once more protest and campaign if the combined efforts of my supporters failed to advance my cause within a reasonable period of time. I put on the prison uniform and left solitary to go to "D" wing which held some 260 lifer and long-term prisoners, including IRA people.

Some weeks later, already into the New Year of 1978, I was disappointed to learn that my letter to "Republican News" was to be censored, despite all my service to the Republican Movement. I was angry at the hypocrisy of the Movement in dedicating itself to liberation for the Irish people while denying freedom of expression to one member of it. I directed a copy of the letter to my local newspaper at home, "The Derry Journal". I expected the "Journal" to publish it in the letters' column and that I would at least have the satisfaction of having expressed the real me to my own people in Derry.

On Friday, February 19th, however, while listening to a London radio station, I was shocked to hear about my letter on the news, and quickly discovered that it was being mentioned on every other news station too. The following day, every national newspaper referred to it. The letter, which the "Journal" had published on its front page, read:

"When I was sixteen, nothing seemed so romantically self-sacrificial as a fight against the odds for an ideal. So I fought. The romantic, self-sacrificial fight could not help being self-satisfying as well. I couldn't help thinking about myself, about what people thought about me when I went into their homes, or to dances, or when I just walked down the street. I couldn't help admiring myself just a wee bit. It was like watching myself on the television of my own mind.

Much later, I was so busy caring for myself, that I couldn't help caring less for others, and when I injured someone, I couldn't think too much about it, because I had to think about myself, about the risks I was taking.

I ignored the human rights of the people I injured, but I was very touchy about my own human rights.

In injuring human beings, I didn't cure injustices, I created new ones.

I didn't realize that my youthful militaristic activities conflicted not only with Christian morality, but also with the principles of democracy and democratic socialism, and I regarded myself as a democratic socialist, don't forget...

But I didn't realize that by engaging in militaristic activities I was repudiating the democratic process and the will of the people, and foisting my will on them. I was in effect telling the people that they didn't know what was good for them, that I knew best. I was almost a little left-wing dictator."

I went on to recommend to all of the parties involved in the conflict, including the British and the loyalist paramilitaries, that they should recognize the problems associated with using violence, should discard it as a tactic, and should embrace the political process wholly.

The refusal to allow my letter into "Republican News" had certainly backfired. After disassociating myself from the IRA, I lost many friends. Many of my fellow IRA prisoners in England ostracized me from that point on. Some verged on wanting to beat me up for speaking my mind. Others, who spent many months in solitary confinement with me, sharing the same small exercise yard for an hour every day, never spoke to me or looked in my direction, though spoke often to prison warders who were locking them up. I was disappointed, but not embittered by this treatment which continued for the next seven years before I was transferred to Northern Ireland. I thought it was a symptom of imprisonment in England where we were all so extremely isolated and dependent on solidarity for survival. This view was confirmed on my eventual return to the Northern Ireland prison system, where people had more respect for views conscientiously held, and where I found the IRA prisoners helpful at all times. Other more broadminded IRA prisoners in England supported me constantly during my long periods in solitary confinement protesting for repatriation to Northern Ireland.

Those who reacted bitterly to my call for Republican engagement in the political process some years later meekly accepted the Republican Movement's decision to take part in elections to the British and Irish parliaments.

I was debating at this time whether or not to try to apologize to the people I had injured via the letter bombs. I had only offered an apology in my speech at the Old Bailey to the "innocent working-class" victims – I had had no intention of apologizing for attacking military or political targets. Since then, however, I had packed in a lot of reading, studying in depth everything from the Documents of Vatican II and the Jerome Biblical Commentary to pacifism and non-violent resistance, human and prisoners' rights. I was quoting much of this material in support of my campaign for repatriation. I hurt me that in relation to almost everything I read, I was not the shining idealist and justice-seeker I'd imagined I was. I was a serious human rights' offender who had fallen for the mystique and aura of the tactic of violence and the old lie, *Dulce Et Decorum Est Pro Patria Mori*.

The Gospels constantly challenged and irritated me, particularly one line in Matthew which read:

> "So, if you are offering your gift at the altar, and there
> remember that your brother has something against
> you, leave your gift there before the altar and go; first
> be reconciled to your brother, and then come and offer
> your gift."

I understood this to mean that religious or liturgical practice was meaningless without some attempt to be reconciled to my victims. Every effort I was making to grab hold of a purer idealism, to change and become a better person, to distance myself from the violence of the past and to wrestle a better future from adversity, was undermined by the fact that I had not addressed the problem of my victims. Nor had I yet addressed the problem of my military and political victims.

Despite the depth of some of my reading material, I simplified whatever I took from it: I saw my violence as having injured not one relationship, but three: my relationship with my victims, my relationship with myself, and any relationship I might try to have with God. I thought that I could sort out the last two if I made a serious attempt, albeit a symbolic one, to address the first.

I had a serious problem with the Catholic Church teaching a Doctrine of the Just War while holding a Gospel which contained precepts like:

> "The old ruling, as you know, was 'an eye for an eye',
> and 'a tooth for a tooth'; but I'm telling you now not to
> retaliate at all against an evil-doer. Rather, if someone
> smacks you on the right cheek, turn and offer him the

other as well. If anyone chooses to sue you for your jacket, let him have your overcoat as well, and whenever an official conscripts you as a bearer for a one mile stint, go with him for two miles... You also know the saying 'Love your neighbor and hate your enemy', but what I tell you now is this: deal lovingly with your enemies and habitually pray for your oppressors, to show that you really are children of your heavenly Father, who causes his sun to rise on the wicked as well as on the good and his rain to fall impartially on all, whether just or unjust. For, if you only show love towards those who deal lovingly with you, what's so meritorious in that? ...What it comes to is that nothing less than perfection will do for you, the perfection of your heavenly Father." (Mt.Ch.5)

It seemed to me that the Catholic Church was inconsistent in its regard for the words of Christ. "This is my Body" and "This is my blood" were taken to be literal and absolute, while "Love your enemies and do good to those who persecute you" was translated into a just war doctrine which effectively allowed you to maim or kill your enemy.

The Just War theory might delineate "just" or "legitimate" targets, but in practice the lines blur. Violence, just or otherwise, escapes every known restraint. The innocent are continually injured or killed by stray bullets or bombs. The best technology cannot restrict the outreach of violence. I was so convinced by my own experience that violence is guaranteed to injure or kill the innocent, that I was being drawn inevitably toward a pacifist position. I could no longer cordon off my attacks on military or political targets as "legitimate" or "just" – I felt that only a pacifist position was truly moral, or truly Christlike. I may have been working on the feeling that only a pacifist outlook would guarantee a conscience free from the guilt of having maimed and hurt people, though active pacifism must mean a lot more than mere abstention from violence.

In common with many prisoners, I was wary of the word "sorry". It could so easily be used hypocritically. I felt, and still feel, that much much more is expressed in deeds than is ever expressed by that word. I inclined then, as now, to the argument of St. James about faith: "Show me your sorrow without deeds, and I will show you my sorrow by my deeds." I don't like it when people ask me if I'm sorry for my past – I'd rather they looked at my deeds for answer.

I had already written at length to the Howard League for Penal Reform about victims' conciliation in response to an article in their Journal, and excerpts from my letters were put together by Martin Wright for inclusion in their newsletter. I was wondering about trying to write to my victims to offer them an apology and something like an explanation. If any of them were living in fear of another IRA attack because they had made statements or appeared in court against me, then I might be able to relieve those worries.

Eventually, I requested Lord Longford to ask the prison system if I would be allowed to write to my victims, and so began a long struggle to win that permission from a reluctant Home Office. British government ministers were set against any prisoner, especially an IRA prisoner, seeking to achieve any kind of moral status beyond that of the gutter.

I had suggested that a mediator should first of all write to my victims to explain that I wished to apologize, and to enquire if they wanted to hear from me – this offered them a choice. I had further stated my view that the mediator should write in such a way as to support and encourage the reconciliation process. After a long struggle, the Home Office stated that I could write to my victims, but only if they wished to hear from me; they appointed the Roman Catholic Chaplain as mediator, and said that he must remain neutral in his letter, not supportive.

Fr. Ennis, though without doubt my best friend in the prison system, was no ordinary priest. He was a full-time member of the Prison Chaplaincy Service, who was classed as a Government Civil Servant and paid as such, who had signed the Official Secrets' Act and was subject to Home Office authority. However, I knew that he did support me, and I agreed to the terms, but I also felt that any victim receiving a bald, cold bureaucratic letter about me would probably throw it away. I needed a letter which was on the side of the process of reconciliation, but I was not getting it. I had to make do.

I was genuinely surprised when just over half of the people injured responded to the mediative letter, one to reject the offer, the rest to accept. One other victim, Reginald Maudling, Home Secretary on Bloody Sunday, had died of natural causes some time before. I wrote off as best I could within the censorship restrictions. I attempted to explain to each person what had motivated me to act as I did, and I apologized wholeheartedly for (depending on the case) intentionally or accidentally injuring or attempting to injure them.

Having kept this whole business absolutely private, I was shocked when, a short time later, a British Sunday newspaper, "The News of the World", ran a story headlined, "Anger As IRA Bomber Says Sorry". The article included photographs of people who, contrary to the implication of the newspaper story, had accepted my apology. One of my victims who had refused to hear from me had evidently taken the story to the newspaper. The gist of the article was that an IRA man was a dirty rotten bastard if he didn't apologize to his victims, and an even dirtier, more rotten bastard if he did. I was embittered by this. No mention was made of the British failure to apologize to hundreds of years worth of Irish victims of British "good neighborliness". Nothing makes me quite as angry as this kind of hypocrisy at which the British media are so expert.

I was taken aback by this treatment and was often questioned by other prisoners, British and Irish, who wanted to know why I'd bothered to apologize. In the next eleven years around and about the prisons, I never met another prisoner who did apologize to his victim(s), and I was not surprised. Once more, some of my fellow IRA prisoners were embittered by my apologies, one telling me that I was mad and required psychiatric treatment.

The prison authorities agreed with this assessment. Out of the blue, I was told I was wanted in the hospital in Wormwood Scrubs. I couldn't find out by whom or for what reason I was wanted. One afternoon I was required to join a group of sex offenders who were going to the hospital for psychiatric assessment. On arrival, I was called to a doctor's office. When I went in, the room was in darkness, with a blinding lamp focused on a chair by the door. A disembodied voice said, "Sit down!" I stood where I was and asked, "Who are you and why do you want to talk to me? Who required me to come to the hospital?" The voice continued to say, "Just sit down! Sit down!" My eyes had now become accustomed to the bright light, and I could see behind it two men holding huge folders of papers. "If you don't want to answer my questions, I don't want to answer yours. Goodbye." I left them to their darkness and returned to "D" wing.

For what turned out to be many years, the prison authorities took the view that everything I had done or said since my conviction at the Old Bailey was an attempt to "pull the wool" over their eyes. I kept on hearing from one or two sympathetic people in the prison system, and from politicians outside who had made representations about me to the Home Office, that I was regarded as too intelligent to be trusted. My ability to endure the long period of solitary confinement naked and without visits was seen as proof that I was some sort of "evil genius" with a long-term plan to trick my way out of the Old Bailey's mountain of life sentences and then single-handedly to subvert the British state!

Another factor added to my series of confrontations with the prison authorities. I had just recently met a number of Irish prisoners who were, I was assured by the IRA prisoners, entirely innocent of their bombing convictions. Initially I could hardly believe the claim, but after meeting and associating with Billy Power and Dickie McIlkenny, and later Paddy Hill, I was convinced that they and the other three men convicted of the Birmingham pub bombings were entirely guiltless. As I heard their detailed stories, I discussed ways in which I thought they might begin to prove their innocence. I offered to try to convince the many prominent people with whom I was in correspondence that they were innocent, and to ask them to visit and help the men. As if this were not enough to earn me enemies in prison system and Home Office, I was also raising the cases of Gerry Conlon of the Guildford Four, and of his father, Giuseppe, who was arrested along with the Maguire family. These cases together amounted to an incredible injustice. I knew the people who had bombed Guildford, and so I knew that the Conlons and Maguires were innocent.

I began to write to prominent people giving them details of the cases and asking them to accept my word that the people concerned were innocent. I stated that I was guilty of my own convictions, and had no problem telling the truth equally about these people. I also interested my lawyer, the brave Gareth Pearce, in them. I kept up this pressure for years, through the bad times when few believed in them, to the better times when their release was inevitable. My action was seen by the closed minds running the prison system as deeply subversive and motivated by the desire to undermine the police and courts...

The effectiveness of my letter-writing on behalf of both myself and the innocent men was such that on one occasion an Assistant Governor of Gartree prison came to my solitary cell to ask how I was getting hold of stamps for my many letters. Since I had been sentenced to successive periods of solitary and loss of all privileges, I should not have been able to purchase stamps from the prison shop for a very long time. I replied that before the start of my protest, I had purchased a large number of stamps with a view to surviving a long period in solitary. The Governor then asked for the exact number of stamps in my possession, so that the prison might know when I was certain to run out of them and cease my correspondence. He said I was a 'poacher in the hedgerows of society', liable to write to everyone. I told him that I was not obliged to answer his question. I felt so concerned about the cases of the innocent men that, upon my release from prison many years later, my first statement to the press concerned the injustice surrounding their continued imprisonment. He then said that he would have me and my cell minutely searched. I answered that there was no guarantee that all of my stamps would be found, and that I would go on posting letters. They searched my cell and found no stamps. However, I continued to send letters and they gave up trying to prevent me.

I was not done with solitary confinement and protest on my own behalf however. My decision to wear the prison uniform and give my supporters a space in which to work constructively for my repatriation proved to have been a wrong one. The Home Office never had any intention of repatriating me, and every letter from a government minister blamed the Northern Ireland office for the decision not to transfer me to a prison nearer home. Meanwhile, letters from the Northern Ireland Office blamed the Home Office. My parliamentary campaigners and others got nowhere. After three years of cooperation with prison rules, I decided to revert to protest once more. I refused prison work in Gartree prison, was placed in solitary, and then refused to leave the solitary wing. I was subsequently sentenced to periods of 56 days in solitary confinement for refusing to leave solitary confinement! This protest went on for some three years.

When any prisoner spent a very long time on solitary protest, he inevitably became something of an institution in the solitary block, and in the prison generally, and I was no exception. The screws might have hated me, but there was a certain comprehensibility and predictability about my existence which may have signaled that excessive and oppressive security was irrelevant. I remember that when I went from the solitary confinement block in Gartree prison to Christmas morning Mass (where, of some four hundred prisoners, only a handful ever entered a church), a prison officer's wife greeted me in the chapel and gave me a Christmas parcel. She used her influence to ensure that I could take it back to my solitary cell. She risked losing her job in the education department of the prison in order to be charitable to me. Her kind act touched me and restored my flagging faith in humanity. I recalled a line I'd read in *Gone With The Wind* to which the prison authorities should have paid attention: 'sugar always caught more flies than vinegar'.

It's a prison rule that things always have to get very bad before they get better. After protesting about an assault on two black prisoners in Long Lartin segregation unit in November, 1983, I was sent to Winson Green prison in Birmingham for a period of solitary, after which I was returned to solitary in Long Lartin. The kindly warders had such treatment in store for me that I had to go to the last line of self-defense in solitary before violence – I mixed excrement and urine and poured it on the hot pipe in my cell, and everywhere else it would go, to keep them at bay. I was sent off for more solitary to Bristol prison over Christmas and New Year.

When I was left alone, I was perfectly behaved, but when warders began to maltreat me I had to choose: I could let them get away with it, in which case it would get much worse, or I could take a stand early on and try to put a stop to it. Unfortunately, it got worse in Bristol and I had to protest. I had applied one morning to have a razor blade during the breakfast period to cut up newspaper articles referring to my case in order to photocopy them for parliamentary correspondence. The small blade was given to me, and I set to work. When the warder who had given me the blade had gone to breakfast, another warder came to my cell and demanded its return. I said I needed it and had been given permission to use it. The warder demanded it once more. I refused to part with it. He went away, rang an alarm bell and awaited the arrival of the riot squad, which he guided to my cell.

The large crowd of warders cowering outside my door with shields, helmets, chin-straps, batons and adrenalin shouted at me to hand over the blade. As I stood there holding the minute razor blade in one hand and a newspaper article in the other, I thought, "Fuck you!" In the tense silence, I held out the blade, squeezed it between my finger and thumb, broke it and threw the minute pieces at their boots. They jumped back in horror and rushed me. I was dragged off to a punishment unit, charged with possession of a weapon, found guilty and sentenced to punishment in solitary. I knew far-off government ministers would exploit this trumped-up charge against my parliamentary supporters, and I was right. I had to decide whether to let the prison warders feel they could freely abuse me, or whether to stop them in their tracks. I chose the latter. I protested to the extent that I was put in a "strip cell" within a cell, with nothing but a wooden board for a bed and a plastic chamber-pot for company. I had to once more spread excrement around the cell and block up the observation slit. I put it to the governor that if I were placed in a normal cell, and if his staff left me alone, my behavior would be normal; if I were not, I would be a thorn in his side which he would not forget for a very long time. He put me in a normal cell, remitting the period of punishment I was supposed to serve for the "weapon" incident.

The work of prison warders is exceptionally dreary and they largely spend their time sitting around drinking tea or coffee, reading pornographic magazines borrowed from prisoners. They also tend to drink beer in their social clubs at lunchtime, and to return to work in the afternoons somewhat the worse for wear and aggressive with it. As a result of the accumulated boredom, the real elixir is action, which produces an appetite for violence. The prospect of a violent assault on a prisoner is something which excites and motivates many prison warders and which supplies fuel for days of retrospective conversation and laughter.

I was reporting all these incidents to my lawyer, Gareth Pearce, who arranged to come to see me in Bristol on Valentine's Day, 1984. At nine o'clock on the morning of her proposed visit, the prison authorities transferred me to Wakefield Prison in Yorkshire, where I received the worst treatment of my fourteen and a half years in prison.

As soon as I arrived in Wakefield, an Assistant Governor met me in reception and told me that I was to be placed in solitary confinement in "F" Wing for the "good order and discipline" of the institution. Governors have the power to place prisoners in indefinite solitary confinement for any reason whatsoever under the "G.O.D." rule. There is no appeal.

As I was being led away, I suddenly realized the implications of his mentioning "F" wing. I remembered that about 1980, the High Court in London had ordered the prison authorities to shut down a notorious "control unit" which had been operating in "F" wing of Wakefield prison. Prisoners had complained about total solitary confinement, extremely restrictive regulations, disorienting wavy lines which had been painted in different colors along the wall of the small exercise yard, etc. The High Court believed them. At the time, when I spoke to prisoners who had been through it, I didn't believe the claim about wavy lines, and I accused people of gross exaggeration. I was wrong.

I was taken to a basement room where there were showers without doors. I was ordered to strip off my clothes and shower in full view of three or four beefy warders. As I did so, my clothes were taken away and replaced with clothes which were sizes too large. I asked why, and was told it was an "F" wing policy. I was then taken to a cell which had a small porch before the metal door. I was told to place my shoes in the porch, and to enter the cell without them. The cell contained nothing but the usual bed cemented to the floor, a chair and a table. The window was the worst I'd ever seen. Set about eight feet up the wall, it was obscured behind rows of bars and had only small blocks of opaque glass beyond. Two blocks were missing and constituted ventilation. The cell was dark.

The warders told me there was a "no-speech" rule, a "no hands in pockets" rule, and rules that included putting the bedding outside the cell every morning at 7am and scrubbing the cell floor on hands and knees using a small scrubbing brush and bucket of water. Since I had not been sentenced to any period of punishment by a Governor or Board or Prison Visitors, I asked for the justification for the series of deviations from the normal solitary rules. The reply was, "You are in "F" Wing and you'll be here for a minimum of two years."

It was clear to me that the control unit was in operation once more under a different name, and that the Wakefield authorities thought they could get away with it for as long as they needed to with certain prisoners. As soon as the warders left, I climbed up to what passed for a window and shouted out the holes. Anyone else in the unit would have heard noises of my arrival and of the new cell door opening. In solitary, it was possible to construct events accurately from the sounds of activity. Two people answered, both friends of mine, one an IRA prisoner and the other a black prisoner from the Spaghetti House siege in London, whom I had known for years.

They told me the regime was designed to break people and that they had been there for some months. They mentioned a London gangster some cells away from me who was in a state of nervous breakdown already, muttering and crying to himself and shouting at times. They also told me he was on heavy doses of psychotropic drugs. We had some banter about how long I would spend there. I joked that I would make sure that the prison authorities would have to move me within eight weeks. The lads laughed heartily and I bet some tuck shop items to back up my promise.

In the morning at 6.30am, warders entered my cell and ordered me to place my bedding outside. I refused, referring to the Prison Rules. The warders charged me with disobeying an order, and also charged me with breaking the "no speech" rule the night before – the actual charge on the sheet was one of shouting. They then ordered me to scrub the cell floor on my hands and knees with a small hand-brush and bucket of filthy water. I said I'd clean the cell in the normal way with the normal tools, mop-bucket and mop, with clean water. They charged me with refusing to obey that order as well and left.

I quickly wrote out two letters, one to my lawyer, Gareth Pearce, and one to my family, describing the conditions and claiming that the control unit was back in business again. In order to be allowed to make allegations in letters about prison treatment, I was required to first of all complain officially about the matter internally to the prison Governor. The catch is that if a complaint is not substantiated by the Prison System inquiring into itself, the prisoner may then be charged with making "false and malicious allegations". Heads the prison wins, tails the prisoner loses. I requested to see the Governor in order to make a number of complaints. The warders told me that if I complained, I would live to regret it.

As I went to get breakfast from a hot-plate outside my cell, I had a plastic plate in one hand and my other hand in my pocket. The warders screamed at me to get my hand out of my pocket. I ignored them and went on to the hotplate. I was refused food for so heinously breaking the "F" wing rules. I replied that I would continue to wear my spare hand wherever I wanted and, if I were being denied food for so doing, then so be it. I returned to my cell without any food. Some minutes later, a plate of nauseating powdered egg with a slice of bread was brought to my cell – minor victory number one to me. The warders were furious, and were threatening to "do" me. I ignored them.

The mini-court case to adjudicate my "offences against prison discipline" was scheduled for 10am. At about ten to ten, I was taken before the Assistant Governor to make my official complaints. I did so, and then handed him my two letters for posting. As I walked back to my cell, the warders were speechless with anger.

Ten minutes later, I was taken before the same Assistant Governor who found me guilty of all the charges against me, ignored my attempts to point to the "control unit" nature of the regime and its contravention of the High Court judgment some years before. He sentenced me to the loss of the privileges which I'd previously illegally lost anyway merely by being in "F'" Wing.

The letters I'd sent out were as time-bombs to the prison authorities. They generally relied on the fact that many prisoners were illiterate, that most prisoners did not campaign for their rights, did not correspond with parliamentarians or lawyers, and were intimidated by the prospect of a long period in solitary confinement. My record should have indicated that I was not that way inclined. They must have known that, once my lawyer and family and friends discovered the nature of the regime, there would be protests in the press and in parliament, with the strong possibility of another application to the High Court. The wavy, disorienting lines were indeed painted along the wall of the exercise yard! They must have known that I was not going to back down, but they ignored completely the impending outcry. They continued charging me with various "offences", and I delighted in the fact that I would have so much evidence of "control unit" regime to use in my case.

Gareth Pearce, my lawyer, visited me from London, and was quite shocked by my appearance and story. Bishop Edward Daly flew from Northern Ireland to see me. I had told him that prisoners in the control unit were being refused the right to attend Mass on Sunday. I had asked to do so, and eventually a non-confrontational priest appeared who proceeded to tell me that he would say a Mass in my cell. I asked him what he would do if ten or twenty other prisoners in the control unit wanted Mass? Spend ten or twenty hours in the unit saying Masses? I said the issue was that prisoners in the unit should be allowed to attend the normal chapel in the normal way. He said he could not help me.

When Bishop Daly arrived, he brought with him the local Bishop Wheeler of Leeds. I described the regime to them and they were shocked also. The next day, Bishop Daly's outrage at my treatment was the lead on the front page of the Northern Ireland newspaper, "The Irish News". The story crossed into some of the British papers, notably "The Guardian", in which I'd originally seen the control unit story years before.

My poor mother visited me, very much against my wishes. I was reluctant to experience the special conditions which Wakefield would undoubtedly apply to my social visits. I was right. I was placed at one end of a very long table between two huge beefy warders. My mother was placed at the far end. She could barely see me, and was on the verge of tears throughout. I was hardly able to maintain a conversation. The warders listened to every word, and sat staring at my mother. I was glad when it was over and deeply embittered against the prison authorities.

Some weeks passed, and I seemed to have run out of steam on my campaign to get out of the control unit. As I was walking along the wavy lines in the exercise yard one day under a gray Yorkshire sky, a warder standing by the gate said to me, "There's an article about you in "The Times" today, right beside the Editorial. They'll have to move you." I couldn't stop and ask him any questions about it, because we were being surveyed by cameras around the yard. I was aching to know more about the article, to know who had written it, and just how far it went, but there was no way of finding out. If information is power, then prisoners are utterly powerless.

That night, I shouted the news to my friends. They reminded me that the eight weeks of my bet were up in a matter of days. I blustered that I was sure I'd be moved out of Wakefield on time to win the bet. I lost it, but one day later I was moved back to Wormwood Scrubs in London. The article in "The Times" had been penned by the former Labor M.P., Phillip Whitehead, who had been helping me for years.

On my way out of Wakefield, one of the escorting warders tried to make amends for the regime and offered a riddle: "D'you know why they had the Famine in Ireland, Paddy?" I didn't answer. "They forgot where they planted the potatoes!" Guffaws of laughter… I don't know why I am made this way, but an insult to my person does not touch me; however, an insulting remark about a tragedy of Irish history is more deeply offensive to me than anything else I can imagine. I had two dreams of violence that recurred for some years, and it is no surprise that one of them was that, in the manner of a contractor taking down a very tall industrial chimney, I pressed a button and blew up Wakefield prison.

I was relieved to be back in the Scrubs. Despite its age, crumbling brickwork and shortage of facilities, it was in London and accessible for visitors, parliamentary and otherwise. "D" Wing, where I was located, contained some 260 lifers and long-termers and there were plenty of friends to choose from. My good friend Fr. Ennis was there, as were some of the Birmingham Six innocent prisoners. Best of all, the Governor of the prison, Ian Dunbar, met me in Reception and said, "I read about you in "The Times" and talked to Fr. Ennis. I told the Home Office I would take you. Don't screw up here." He had caused some waves himself by writing to "The Times" and referring to prisons as "penal dustbins". He treated me well, and I responded well.

I had by now served almost nine years in prison, and I was still on Category A – the top security rating for prisoners whose potential escape was regarded as dangerous to the State. I knew English prisoners quite well who had been convicted of one or more murders and yet who had been decategorized within a year or two of their conviction. I felt that I should fight the categorization, though with little prospect of success. I wrote to various supporters and spoke to Ian Dunbar about it. Dunbar had courage. He often wandered around "D" Wing's four floors, visiting top security prisoners in their cells during the day or evening when they had association together, where he'd ask questions and debate matters. He was exceptionally gifted within the many limitations imposed upon him by the Home Office and reactionary, unthinking prison staff. The efforts of Father Gerry Ennis on my behalf were quite inestimable too.

A year after my arrival in Wormwood Scrubs, where I'd had no trouble, I was suddenly told that my security category had been changed to "B", and that I was being transferred to Blundeston Prison in Suffolk. I was "ghosted" out during the lunch-hour, when everyone was locked up, and so had no time to say goodbye to anyone. "D" Wing's Principal Officer, who gave me the news, told me that he'd recommended against my decategorization, and that he felt sure I'd escape, or attempt to escape, from Blundeston. He thought me an unrepentant cad, he said. He was a pretty typical prison warder, bigoted to the last and wrong as well.

Ian Dunbar met me in Reception before I left and took me into an office. He said, "O'Doherty, I have taken a tremendous risk in backing your decategorization. If you screw up in Blundeston, or if you escape or anything like that, heads will roll here and in the Home Office. If you mess up, no other Irish prisoner will get the same break. Remember that. The prison staff in Blundeston will have to be reassured by you that you are not a danger – I cannot help you there. Good luck." I thanked him and set off in a prison van without, for the first time, gun-toting policemen in cars whose sirens and motorcycle outriders scared other drivers to the sides of the roads. This time I travelled with no more than three prison officers. I couldn't believe it was happening to me. I owed a lot to the courage of people like Ian Dunbar, who tried to be radical within the system.

Blundeston was situated in beautiful countryside beside a lake, and a few miles only from Great Yarmouth on the seafront. My arrival was greeted by shocked silence. Some life sentence prisoners were fearful my arrival marked a security upgrade for the prison generally. This led them to believe that their presence in Blundeston might not, after all, indicate progress towards release. I told them that I had been decategorized, and they began to relax, and recalled that one other Irish political prisoner, Peter Short, had already been through Blundeston.

I was called into an office to be questioned by prison warders. One said, "There isn't much security here, just a wire fence, rickety in places. Our wives are worried that the IRA is going to land in here, blow the place up, and enable your escape. What about that?"

I tried to tell them that it was not unusual for IRA volunteers to cease to volunteer for whatever reason. I was one such former member, and I no longer had any support for violence. I wanted to be left alone. I assured them that if they gave me no trouble, I would give them none. They came up with the old lie, "We thought that once a member of the IRA, always a member."

I replied with a series of questions: "Who would join the IRA if no-one could ever leave it? What community in Northern Ireland would support a locally-recruited paramilitary if none of that community's fathers, sons or daughters could ever leave it? What secret organization would endanger its security by forcibly keeping within its ranks people who did not want to be there?"

That, and my general demeanor, seemed to convince them. I was happy enough in Blundeston, surprised by its rose-bushes, flowers, greenery and nearby lake. Six months later, in September 1985, when I had served exactly ten years in England, I was told I was to be transferred to a Northern Ireland prison.

On the morning of my transfer, my confidence was boosted by the news that I was being sent to Birmingham airport in an ordinary taxi with only two warders for security. I felt better about myself and about the future.

One of the escorting warders, with an embarrassed air, handed me something. It was a religious paperback book which he and his wife had gotten for me, and which bore a kind inscription, including the information that they had been praying for me for months, and would continue to do so. As I prepared to leave England after a decade in those factories where offenders are slowly but surely fashioned into victims, I recalled the occasions when prison officers' wives or prison governors' wives had shown me kindness and had helped thereby to undo the evil the prison system was practicing on me. Assistant Governor Deane's Welsh wife in Wormwood Scrubs had taught a brilliant English literature class, and had created a small but sovereign kingdom where prisoners were allowed to be human for an hour or two every day.

The journey to the airport was uneventful, and in the airport security area, I listened to Irish radio as it headlined my transfer. The flight was equally uneventful, and I recalled the flight from Ireland ten years before aboard the Royal Air Force jet, and my fears then that I might never see Ireland again. I was almost happy for the first time in a decade. My arrival, however, was a blow to everything built up so far.

CHAPTER 8

A Bitter Fruit

At Belfast airport, armed police and soldiers clambered up the aisle of the plane to our back row, placed handcuffs on me and took me off in a veritable orgy of security. Police jeeps, army jeeps, and an armored car, troops and police waited on the tarmac. I was shoved into the armored car and taken off in a convoy to Long Kesh prison. I tried to protest that my security rating had been downgraded back in England, but they laughed that off, saying that the Northern Ireland Office would make up its own mind independently.

The authorities in the prison seemed totally convinced of my evil dangerousness. Long Kesh was effectively run by Republican and Loyalist paramilitaries, who controlled their respective wings and men. An Assistant Governor expected me to go to the IRA-run wings. I told him I had no intention of doing so, that I was no longer a member of the IRA and that I wished to owe it no favors. He then said they had really nowhere else to put me, since there was basically only a wing of sex offenders with two or three Protestant Loyalist paramilitary prisoners who had had disagreements on the Loyalist-run wings and a couple of Republicans with similar pedigree. He was sure I wouldn't want to associate with sex offenders and Loyalists, in that order. I said I wanted to go to that wing, but he put me in solitary overnight. Again in the morning, I was asked if I wanted to go to the IRA wings. I refused, and was eventually taken to the "mixed" wing.

The prominent Loyalist prisoners who met me, "Junior" McClelland and "Rab" Turner, greeted me in a guardedly friendly manner. They began to tell me that, once off the paramilitary-controlled wings, they were constantly harassed by prison warders who hadn't the courage to maltreat them anywhere else. They warned me to be on my guard. Within minutes of this conversation, Rab had been charged by a warder with using foul language, and was removed to solitary pending his adjudication the following morning. I saw and heard that he had not used any foul language, and I offered to go witness in his support. Rab beat the charge, and we three began to build some solidarity. John Dornan and Stevie Berry, the latter a former INLA leader, were a great help to me also. Within a few months, when many other disaffected men on the paramilitary wings saw that we could survive off them, our numbers on the mixed wings began to grow.

I had nothing but trouble in Long Kesh prison from one day to the next. I was too well versed in British and European rules on the treatment of prisoners, and constantly referred the authorities to regulations which were supposed to govern their behavior. They were not used to having someone who constantly corresponded with prominent people about every incident of penal life. It is no exaggeration to record that Long Kesh hated me absolutely. I found the religious bigotry and discrimination as bad as in Crumlin Road prison a decade before. Since I constantly encouraged prisoners on the mixed wings to employ lawyers, write to M.P.s, and stand up for their rights, I was probably the least popular prisoner. The final straw must have been my interest in the case of the "UDR 4". These young members of the Ulster Defense Regiment had been convicted of the murder of a Roman Catholic. I talked to two of them and found their denials, their stories and details of police misbehavior very credible. I helped one of them in particular to frame a letter about their case, and gave him many names and addresses of persons who would at the very least investigate their claims. Since then, three of the four have been released, and one remains in prison. The prison authorities were not overjoyed that members of the Ulster Defense Regiment were accusing the Royal Ulster Constabulary of irregularities, and my slight involvement was once more regarded as proof that I was only interested in undermining the forces of law and order, etc.

Within two years, there were so many people on the mixed wings that the authorities announced they were going to open a new prison, Maghaberry, which had been moth-balled for years. No paramilitary prisoners were to be sent there, it was said. One night virtually everyone I knew on the mixed wings was given paper sacks and told to pack their belongings ready for transfer to the new Maghaberry prison in the morning. They all went, and I was left behind. I was told that I was still regarded as high security and would not be moved. I wrote a letter to a member of the House of Lords about this and related matters, and applied to see an Assistant Governor to have it posted. I did not trust posting letters through the normal channels run by prison warders, since so many of my letters "went missing" and were never received.

When I raised the various matters with the Assistant Governor and asked him to make an official note recording that I was posting a parliamentary letter, he took it and threw it across the table onto the floor. He said he would record nothing and told me to take the letter away and give it to prison warders as normal. When I refused and made to leave the office, a Principal Officer locked the door to prevent me. I sat down for five or more minutes, looking at my letter on the floor, until they let me leave. Right outside the office, I met a chaplain who knew that I had been having problems posting parliamentary letters, but who still had some doubts. I was able to tell him right away about the Assistant Governor throwing my letter on the floor, and he went into the office to enquire about it. Some minutes later, he came to my cell and told me that he had no further doubts about my claims of harassment and interference with correspondence. My letter had been on the floor as I'd said, and the Assistant Governor had not denied it. He said he'd raise with various authorities the very many problems stemming from my location in Long Kesh. I was given paper sacks the same evening and told to prepare for transfer to Maghaberry the next morning.

I got to Maghaberry, but the same securenoia prevented me even leaving the "houses" to go to work with all the other prisoners. There were some excellent courses in trades' skills available, but I was given nominal work on the wing, cleaning a shower unit and bathroom. I protested as much as possible that my English security rating had been ignored in Northern Ireland and that it was absurd that I was being kept on "high security" while many life sentence prisoners, with multiple murders to their credit and ten years or more spent on paramilitary wings, were regarded as medium security. My arguments cut no ice. The Governor of Maghaberry, Duncan McLachlan, proved to be the most helpful and constructive person around. He was dedicated to running Maghaberry along radically modern lines, but had to hasten slowly in order to ensure the prison staff were following his lead. He eventually told me I was medium security, and gave me a prime job touch-typing and word-processing in a Braille Unit.

The regular contact I gained with my family, friends, and community representatives back in Northern Ireland was infinitely more rehabilitative than anything the penal system could ever have produced in me by force. Seeing my septuagenarian mother, a pensioner and widow, for years exhausted by travelling hundreds of miles to an unfriendly prison in England for a visit behind oppressive security, was deeply enraging, particularly since soldiers or policemen who committed crimes in Northern Ireland were granted instant transfers to England.

Imprisonment of Irish Republican prisoners in English prisons is totally counter-productive and excessively punitive. As an isolated and maltreated group, their protests often upset the entire prison system. They feel their innocent families are subject to the totally unjustified punishment of having to traipse around England to try to keep up with them when they are constantly transferred between prisons. The Northern Ireland prison system is currently equipped both physically and psychologically to cope with paramilitary prisoners in a way that need not aggravate or demean either side, and I feel very strongly that Irish Republican prisoners should be transferred to Northern Ireland. I am sure the English prisons would heave a huge sigh of relief to be rid of them, and the prisoners' family relationships would be strengthened by their repatriation. Bitterness between the IRA and the British Government would be diminished.

When men are cut off from their families and communities they lose touch with political developments and changes which everyone else regards as natural and normal. As a result, they are caught in an embittered time-warp and the prison system consequently expends vast amounts trying to cope with them by means of greater and more oppressive security. Strengthening links between prisoners and their families and communities is a necessary element of progress towards a settlement in Northern Ireland.

The Life Sentence Review Board had assessed my case in 1986, 1987 and 1988 but did not recommend the fixing of a release date. By 1989, I had served fourteen years. A considerable head of steam had begun to build up across the entire community in Northern Ireland about the length of life sentences being served by political prisoners, and my case (as someone serving a non-homicidal life sentence, for offences excluding murder) was getting a great deal of attention. The International Red Cross, on its annual visit to Northern Ireland prisons, became particularly interested and sent a lawyer, Cristina Pellandini, to spend a lunch period locked up in my cell with me, going over relevant papers and news cuttings. Nobel Peace Prize winner, Mairead Corrigan-Maguire, was a regular visitor to me from the Peace People in Belfast, and a leading lawyer, Joe Rice, had been representing me. Finally, in 1989, at the fourth attempt, a release date was fixed in my case, and approved by the Secretary of State for Northern Ireland.

It took me, in all, fourteen and a half years to get out of the British prison system. For the sake of comparison, it is instructive to look at the case of British soldier, Private Ian Thain, who was convicted in Northern Ireland of the murder of a young Catholic lad, Kidso Reilly, whom he shot in the back. Thain served less than two years of a life sentence, was released back into the British Army, got back-pay for his time in prison, and was given a gun to hold once more – a monument to British Justice! There were no tabloid newspaper outcries about his failure to apologize, nor about the brevity of his sentence, nor questions to him about his victim's relatives...

I was finally released from a Northern Ireland prison in September, 1989, in time to begin full-time studies for a Pure English degree at Trinity College, Dublin, and to work as a freelance journalist to keep the wolf from the door.

I left behind not only former IRA friends, but former UDA and UVF Protestant paramilitary friends. We had discovered in prison that we were so similar. We learned to trust each other, and became friends, but too late for many of our victims. This has led me to oppose the Churches, Catholic and Protestant, who demand that Catholic and Protestant children must be educated apart and never play or learn together. I met many men in prison, Catholic and Protestant, who had never met a person of the opposing community until they shot one. It is hypocritical of Catholic and Protestant Church leaders to constantly lament the killings on both sides, while they are the cause of religious apartheid in Northern Ireland schools and a primary cause of the social division. Prisons are belatedly doing for political/religious opponents what the schools should have done for a long time before, namely introducing them...

The fact that Northern Ireland politics and politicians are so deadened and backward-looking does not encourage young people to avoid or leave paramilitaries where they find a sense of action, a potential to change events and conditions, and patriotic traditions which go back for decades. If young people see a bankrupt political gerontocracy as the only alternative to paramilitarism, then there is little hope of weaning them away from the "physical force" tradition.

Journalists often ask me, "What about your victims?" The enquiry is never motivated by an actual concern about my victims (if it was, the question would be addressed directly to them), but rather by the desire to acquire a poorly-phrased or unguarded response from me which might be turned into a lurid headline or paragraph. Other questions follow, "How do you think they feel about your going to university/about your writing a book/about your getting on with your life?" or whatever. How would I know? Am I qualified in remote telepathic diagnosis? If I had no feelings toward my victims, I would never have addressed public and private apologies to them.

For all that I might pathologically and megalomaniacally imagine myself to be the cause of every evil that ever happened in Northern Ireland, the fact is that the specters which haunt us from history and politics dwarf any individual in the conflict, whether he be a soldier shooting dead an unarmed Catholic or an IRA volunteer setting off a bomb in London. The situation is greater than any individual participating in it. I would be failing in my duty to myself and everyone else if I imploded on feelings of guilt and lived off the dole or 'the sick' for the rest of my life. I see everyone as having been victimized by the situation, and I do not discriminate between Protestant or Catholic, British or Irish victims. In my view, the kid in a paramilitary whose life is going to be lost in a shooting or who is going to prison for ten or twenty years is also a victim, a victim of a different kind from the innocent person injured or maimed, but a victim none the less. It is not lost on me that by accepting the police offer of a deal, society might only have required of me three years in prison, but I have had to deal with over fourteen years spent in confinement.

A former long-term prisoner has to overcome both his imprisonment and his past; he has to make a success of becoming a citizen dedicated to the public good. The most positive interpretation of imprisonment – alongside all the negative ones of punishment, societal revenge, long-term maltreatment – is that it should equip a person to rebuild a useful life. I have studied, passed exams and spent five years at a university. I have worked a various jobs, including journalism, to supplement my meager student funding and in order to pay bills. I haven't ever signed on the dole or been a burden to the taxpayer (except when I was a very expensive burden in the top security prison system). The fact that I have worked and got my life together is a positive thing and an encouragement to others coming out of prison behind me; it should also be an inspiration to those in penology or criminology who believe that prisons should not be factories where offenders are slowly tortured into victims, and where their capacity to live normal lives is destroyed. I don't feel I have to apologize for trying to build a useful life.

I am committed to trying to encourage a peaceful settlement of the conflict surrounding British/Irish relations. Since my release, and contrary to the many voices raised against it, I have not bombed, shot or felt hatred toward anyone. I don't know of a single released life sentence prisoner from the Northern Ireland conflict who has gotten into any trouble at all.

I have tried to encourage parties to talk for peace, and have written articles for the press or made radio and television programs with the same end in mind. To my mind, it is lunatic to try to make peace without involving the paramilitaries who are making the war and who can, with a single bomb or bullet, tear down a political framework which has been erected without their participation. Both states, the Republic of Ireland and Northern Ireland, owe their formation to violence and threat of violence, and to violent men, and both states revere their memory. The history of British interference in Irish affairs is nothing if not violent!

I have constantly expressed the view on television and radio that there is a path to peace in Northern Ireland. It seems to me that all three sides to the conflict share an equal measure of responsibility for it. It is a figment of British propaganda that the IRA is responsible for all of the violence in Northern Ireland.

The first murder committed in my youth was the killing of a Roman Catholic, Peter Ward, by the Protestant paramilitary organization, the Ulster Volunteer Force, when I was eleven years old, and three years before the IRA was even re-formed. The first bombs to explode in Northern Ireland in these troubles were not IRA bombs, but Protestant paramilitary bombs aimed against the government of Terence O'Neill, who had secured a reputation of one bent on the establishment of better relations with the Republic of Ireland and with Catholics in Northern Ireland.

The first policeman, the first soldier, the first minister of religion, the first politician, and the first lawyer killed in Northern Ireland were all killed by Protestant Loyalist paramilitaries. The Protestant Royal Ulster Constabulary still harbors within its ranks not only the hidden killers of innocent Roman Catholics, but also those officers involved more recently in the "shoot-to-kill" murders of unarmed IRA or INLA volunteers, murders which the British police chief, John Stalker, attempted to investigate until the intelligence services decided to block him.

While the IRA is usually described as engaging in terrorist violence, the British Government's armed forces have engaged in what can only be described as terrorist violence before, during and after Bloody Sunday, and have many controversial murders and shootings to their name. The British Prime Minister made history recently when he admitted the innocence of the thirteen Civil Rights marchers who were shot and killed by British army paratroopers on Bloody Sunday, 1972. It is the first time that the British Government has admitted committing an atrocity in Ireland similar to the IRA's atrocities in Enniskillen, when innocent people gathering to commemorate war dead were blown up and killed, and in Birmingham when twenty-one innocent people enjoying an evening out in bars were blown up and killed. Since so many people joined the IRA in response to the Bloody Sunday murders, the British must take proportionate responsibility for the strengthening of the IRA, and for its persistence over a quarter of a century. There is a lot of evidence that members of the British security forces have colluded with Protestant Loyalist paramilitaries who both killed selected persons within Northern Ireland and attacked targets in the Republic of Ireland. One officer of the SAS has been identified as the gunman who shot dead an IRA officer in the Republic of Ireland, before he himself was captured and shot dead by the IRA in Northern Ireland. All this, and the frenzied SAS shootings of unarmed IRA volunteers in Gibraltar and elsewhere, together with the wrongful conviction and imprisonment of many innocent Irish people for up to fifteen years in England, add up to a sorry British record in Ireland.

As the past quarter of a century has shown, the IRA is not going to be beaten by any so-called security solution imposed by a British Government in Ireland. The Protestant Loyalist population of Northern Ireland is not going to be dominated or defeated by IRA violence. The British will not be beaten back to their own country by the fleabites of the IRA campaign. Until all parties to the conflict agree to talk about how to make a lasting peace, there will be a lasting war in Northern Ireland, spreading irregularly to other parts of Britain and Ireland.

The longest break the people of Northern Ireland have had from most of the violence was the period of the 1974/75 ceasefire, when the British Government, for the second time in two years, talked directly to the IRA about a path to peace. Protestant Churchmen, motivated by the Gospel and needing no other license, instigated that ceasefire. British Government arguments that it is not possible to talk to those who use violence in support of political objectives (by which it singles out the IRA) are utterly hypocritical in view of the many acts of British violence in pursuit of British policy in Northern Ireland and in view of the talks which have already taken place.

No side has the right to hijack the high moral ground and claim that it is too good to talk to the other side(s). Each side has bloody hands, and everyone has a responsibility to prevent the loss of human life and the destruction of the quality of life in Northern Ireland and elsewhere resulting from the conflict. Those who refuse to talk a way to peace imply that superior violence, with total surrender of the other sides, is the only real avenue to it. We have seen the consequences of decades of violence on all sides and the consequences of trying, in vain, to find a solution through a bankrupt political gerontocracy.

The sacredness of a single human life and the desire to safeguard it should outweigh any argument against talking to paramilitaries. I believe that talking to paramilitaries – the people who are fighting the war – is the way to peace. The path to the future is paved either with the courage to talk, or with bullets, bombs and bodies. I prefer talks.

Epilogue

During my time in prison, I was constantly seeking to know what was right and, not surprisingly, what was wrong. I studied, reflected, prayed and also found the courage to look honestly at my own past acts, without the false comforts of peer group support or borrowed ideology. I took sole responsibility for what I had done in the name of Irish freedom, and reflected upon my actions, upon what I alone had done.

Whether in the most basic terms of respect for every person's human rights, or whether in light of the teachings of the Gospel, I could not justify political violence and the rationalised injury or killing of my fellow human beings. It was uncomfortable to recognise that I was a human rights' violator.

I could plainly see that if 'freedom fighters' could not offer unqualified respect for human rights and human lives during their struggle, then who could possibly ever trust them to respect human rights and lives when in power? How could there be a transformation of the readiness to maim or kill subsequent to the moment of achievement of political power?

We had gone to war in Ireland in a hurry, and had never explored or tried any democratic or political means. In fact, right at the beginning of our struggle, we had refused to recognise the parliaments of Northern Ireland and the Irish Republic, thereby walking Irish Republicans into a *cul de sac* from which the only exit involved a 360° reversal of beliefs some twenty years later. We declared war before we ever tried to struggle politically, democratically, peacefully and through that declaration of war, many people were needlessly to lose their lives.

As someone from a Catholic background and culture, I was completely convicted by the person of Jesus in the Gospels. I remember reading Paul VI's *'Paenitemini'*, about the concept of conversion and repentance. It made the point that evil action – or sin, if I may still use that word in the third millennium – had three consequences: it destroyed the relationship between the doer and the community; it destroyed the relationship between the doer and his inner self; it destroyed the relationship between the doer and God...

In total solitary confinement in prison, the damage to my relationship with the community was clear; my unhappiness about my own human rights' record destroyed my inner conscience; I felt that I had estranged myself from God.

The only way back was to firstly admit the wrongness of my deeds, both privately and publicly. This on its own required a lot of courage and tenacity, since it would be painful for many of my friends who were still dedicated to the armed struggle and had not reflected as I had. But even more, it required that I should recognise the existence of my victims, and should somehow make an effort – even if only a symbolic effort – to address the wrongs done to them. I decided to write my views to my local paper in Derry, Northern Ireland, which I later did. I fought for the right to write letters of apology to my victims, which I later did. I sought the forgiveness of my victims, and then later, the forgiveness of God.

My comrades in prison thought I was mad! They could more easily have tolerated any rationalised political arguments against the armed struggle, but the mention of religious faith, the Gospels and God were wholly repulsive, and I was totally ignored thereafter by many of them for years.

I was released after fourteen years in prison, and was not subject to the national media censorship which continued for another five years. I never hesitated in print, radio and on television to call for an end to violence and an engagement with the democratic process. I was quite prominent for a few years in this work.

Later, the movement composed of Sinn Fein and the IRA closely mirrored the personal transformation I had undergone, when they addressed three issues: they finally publicly expressed sorrow for the sufferings caused, put their weapons' arsenal beyond use, and dedicated themselves wholly to the democratic process. This transformation opened their way to full participation in democratic national politics.

There is no doubt that the September 11 attacks in the USA finally depicted armed struggle for what it ultimately is: a process whereby human lives may be destroyed in a rationalised, calculated manner for political ends. Such rationalised calculation is intrinsically evil, and there is only one way back from it – to repent entirely of it. The September 11 attacks devastated many Irish people in America and Ireland who had formerly supported armed struggle, and who thereafter were moved to distance themselves entirely from it.

And so the years continue to pass... I remember and reflect every day on the past – going over in my mind that many teenage friends gave their lives in the armed struggle, and took lives in it also. I constantly think of lost lives and suffering on all sides – these thoughts never leave me. I try to make sense of thirty years of war and I conclude that the essential lesson of my life is this: the moment that I, as a young, idealistic justice-seeker employed violence in support of my noble cause, I became a serious human rights' violator and brought dishonour and shame on my cause and on myself. I became mired in sin. A cause so served becomes drenched in blood and is no longer noble.

The only political ideology that is worthy of association with a noble cause is one which offers unconditional respect for the rights and life of every human person.

I offer my story to you in the hope that some young person might, in reading it, avoid the choices I made when I was but 15 yrs of age, and their horrible consequences.

The Author has created a Web site to amplify various references in "The Volunteer" which readers might like more fully explained. Readers may also browse many photographs made available there. See:

www.iravolunteer.com

CPSIA information can be obtained at www.ICGtesting.com
Printed in the USA
BVOW08s0007101215

429721BV00004B/148/P